IN THE
BLOOD

ANNE HOLLAND has written numerous non-fiction books re-
lating to horse racing, including *The Grand National – The Irish at
Aintree*, published by The O'Brien Press, and *Steeplechasing:
A Celebration of 250 Years*. She was also a successful amateur rider.
Anne lives in rural Westmeath and hunts regularly.

Other books by Anne Holland include:

THE GRAND NATIONAL The Irish At Aintree
HORSES FOR COURSES An Irish Racing Year
BEST MATE The Illustrated Story of
the Nation's Favourite Racehorse
HUNTING, A Portrait
STEEPLECHASING A Celebration of 250 Years
DRUGS AND HORSES
RIDING IN A POINT-TO-POINT
CLASSIC HORSE RACES
A PRACTICAL GUIDE TO HUNTING
STRIDE BY STRIDE The Illustrated Story of Horseracing
GRAND NATIONAL the Official Celebration of 150 Years
DAWN RUN the Story of a Champion Racehorse
and her Remarkable Owner

CONTENTS

First published 2009 by The O'Brien Press Ltd,
12 Terenure Road East, Rathgar, Dublin 6, Ireland.
Tel: +353 1 4923333; Fax: +353 1 4922777
E-mail: books@obrien.ie
Website: www.obrien.ie

ISBN: 978-1-84717-180-1
Text © copyright Anne Holland 2009
Copyright for typesetting, layout, editing, design
© The O'Brien Press Ltd

1 2 3 4 5 6 7 8
09 10 11 12 13 14

Printed and bound in Poland by Białostockie Zakłady Graficzne S.A.
The paper in this book is produced using pulp from managed forests.

ACKNOWLEDGEMENTS

With grateful thanks for time, care and help, I am indebted to the following, with special thanks for
proofreading to Martin Murphy of Horse Racing Ireland:

Arthur Barker; Sean Bell; Jim Bolger; Emma Byrne, designer, and Helen Carr, editor, The O'Brien
Press; Coolmore; Richard, Duc De Stacpoole; Tamarisk Doyle (Horse Racing Ireland); Jim Dreaper;
Michael Forde; Tom Gallagher; Tucker Geraghty; Sandra Ginnelly, Galway Races; Brian Graham; Sir
Henry Grattan-Bellew; Buster Harty; Eddie Harty Senior; Eddie Harty Junior; Liam Healy; Pat
Healy; Emmeline Hill; Jeremy Hill; Horse Racing Ireland; Yasmin Hyde; Kildorrery Tourist Office;
Michael Knightly; Gail List; Martin Molony; Peter Molony; Joan Moore; Jonathan Moore; Mullins
Family; Martin Murphy; Michael and Ivan O'Brien; Peter O'Hehir; Tony O'Hehir; John and
Caitriona Oxx; *The Racing Post*; Leo Powell; Brendan Sheridan; Jim Sheridan; Tony Sweeney; *The
Irish Field*; Gay Veitch; Charlie Vigors; Nicky Vigors; Austin Walsh; Tom and Noreen Walsh; Walsh
Family; Tom Walshe; Dermot Weld; John Weld; Olive Whelan; Guy St John Williams.

A.H.

IN THE BLOOD

IRISH RACING DYNASTIES

ANNE HOLLAND

THE O'BRIEN PRESS
DUBLIN

Left: Dan Moore, patriarch of the Moore and Carberry families, seen here riding Revelry. Dan was a fine amateur rider and top class trainer like his son, Arthur; his daughter Pamela married Tommy Carberry and riders Paul, Philip, Thomas, Nina and Peter John Carberry are his grandchildren.

Below: At Fairyhouse in April 2007 there were four members of the Carberry family in action during the day, (L-R) Philip, Nina, Peter John and Paul. It was left to Paul on his first day back from injury to ride a winner aboard Aitmatov.

INTRODUCTION

GENERATIONS OF IRISH FAMILIES HAVE HORSE-RACING BLOOD coursing through their veins; it is a thread that links diverse equine and human characters, past and present. The people and horses portrayed here represent only the tip of the iceberg of all those who love and are committed to horse-racing. In addition to families – owners, trainers, jockeys, breeders and others whose lives revolve around racing – a number of favourite horses are included; again, they represent but a small part of the whole. Ireland may be a tiny dot on the globe, yet it is the third largest breeder of thoroughbred horses in the world.

It is a privilege and pleasure to have met many of the families, to hear their interesting stories and I thank them all. Many are worthy of a whole book to themselves.

✦ ✦ ✦

Above: Familial pride: Paul Carberry congratulates his sister Nina after she won the Fred Winter hurdle at the Cheltenham Festival on 20-1 shot Dabiroun in 2005.

Below: Locals turn out in force to welcome home Grand National hero Bobbyjo and his trainer, Tommy Carberry, in 1999; the horse was ridden by Paul Carberry and it was the first Irish-trained winner since L'Escargot, trained by Dan Moore and ridden by Tommy, in 1975.

Opposite: Mud pack! A delighted Nina Carberry smiles after she won the BGC P.P. Hogan Memorial Cross Country Chase on Garde Champetre for trainer Enda Bolger at Punchestown in February 2008.

The Carberrys and the Moores, for example, have exemplary racing and training pedigrees. Dan Moore was beaten by a short head in *Battleship*'s 1938 Grand National, riding *Royal Danielli*; and he trained *L'Escargot* to win the great race in 1975. His son Arthur is a successful trainer too, and both father and son were good riders. Tommy Carberry started off as an apprentice to Dan Moore and went on to win the Aintree Grand National both as a jockey and as a trainer (*L'Escargot* and *Bobbyjo*). He married Dan and Joan Moore's daughter, Pamela, and their children are Thomas, Paul, Philip, Mark, Nina and Peter John;

Opposite top left: Kevin Prendergast with his stable jockeys at Leopardstown in 2006, champions both: leading professional jockey Declan McDonagh, left, and apprentice champion Chris Hayes.

Opposite top right: P.J. Paddy (Darkie) Prendergast.

Opposite bottom: Patrick Prendergast with Waterways, *a winner at The Curragh in 2005.*

Above: The legendary rider Pat Taaffe, right, with his son, Tom in 1982.

Bottom right: Tom Taaffe seen here in 2005 with his Cheltenham Gold Cup hero, Kicking King *after the horse had won the Guinness Chase at Punchestown.*

Paul and Philip are both top-flight National Hunt jockeys, while Nina is considered the first lady of Irish jumping and an excellent ambassadress for the sport. A natural athlete, she also has a racing brain, which she uses to great effect against experienced rivals. When Paul won the Grand National on *Bobbyjo*, trained by his father Tommy, in 1999, they became the sixth father / son, trainer / jockey pairing to win the famous race; they were followed in this feat by Ted and Ruby Walsh, with *Papillon*, in the 2000 Grand National. Dan Moore's brother, Andrew, had thirteen daughters including Kate who married Jack Leonard of Culmullen, Co. Meath, whose son Hugh Leonard, a renowned Meath horseman, was also a successful amateur rider, and his son, Eddie Leonard, was European champion apprentice in 1987.

P.J. 'Darkie' Prendergast was a top trainer too, as were his sons Kevin and Paddy. Kevin, now in his seventies, is still training, while Paddy is retired. Paddy's son Patrick is now a trainer in his own right. 'Darkie' was apprenticed to James Daly, of Liffeybank, in 1926 or 1927, and later his indentures transferred to Tom Coombs, for whom he rode winners.

Thereafter he went to England, riding numerous NH winners for Epsom trainers up to 1936, when he emigrated to Australia, where Kevin was born. 'Darkie' took out his Irish trainer's licence in 1940 and the rest, as they say, is history.

In 1963 Kevin Prendergast first took out a trainer's licence, having been an amateur rider of repute (about two hundred winners) and assistant trainer, first in Australia and then to his father. In the nearly fifty years since, he has won the 2,000 Guineas with *Nebbiolo*, the Irish 2,000 Guineas, and the Irish 1,000 Guineas twice. He has also won the Irish St Leger four times.

The Taaffes, too, are a timeless part of Irish racing: Pat won the Grand National twice on the Vincent O'Brien-trained *Quare Times* in 1955 and on *Gay Trip*, trained by Fred Rimell, in 1970; he will forever be associated with the great *Arkle* after their stunning Cheltenham Gold Cup treble, and to most who witnessed him the greatest steeplechaser of all time.

Pat's son Tom Taaffe is a trainer based near Straffan in Co. Kildare; he trained the 2005 Gold Cup winner, *Kicking King*. His young son, Pat, may well be another chip off the old block, and who better for him to glean tips from than the outstanding Ulsterman Tony McCoy who in 2009 notched up his three thousandth winner!

This is a book that is hard to finish, because new family members are coming along all the time ... I am sorry that it has not been possible to include many other deserving families in this one volume – but I dedicate it to all the wonderful people who share the consuming passion that is Irish horse racing.

Vive le sport!

Opposite: All set for the future: Pat Taaffe junior with all-time champion NH jockey (A.P.) Tony McCoy.

Above: A model racehorse in every way, Arctic Storm, *born 1959, with his devoted lad Tommy Forde*

FROM ARCTIC STORM TO SEA THE STARS

A WEAK SUN FILTERS THROUGH THE POCKETS of mist early in the morning on the Curragh, that oasis in the heart of Kildare dotted with sheep and studded with gorse; fluffy white clouds scud overhead while alongside, commuters are buzzing along the new motorway to reach their Dublin offices, oblivious to the strings of racehorses a stone's throw away. Out among the brilliant yellow gorse clumps, with the racecourse grandstand silhouetted in the background, it is peace and tranquillity – apart from the occasional squeal and buck, and the banter among the lads and lasses, joking about their exploits last night or laughing when someone falls off.

It is part and parcel of the Irish racing tradition that has taken place on 'the Curragh Plains of Kildare', that near 5,000-acre expanse of naturally springy, well-drained turf that makes it Ireland's natural headquarters of racing and training since the mid-1600s. Riding out on a fit thoroughbred on a beautiful morning, the wind in the face, the turf flicking below, is poetry in motion, there is no other place to match it in the world.

30 June 1962 is indelibly imprinted in the memory of John Oxx. He was just a few days

short of his twelfth birthday, and his trainer father, also John, was to run their 20-1 Irish 2,000 Guineas winner *Arctic Storm* in the Irish Derby; young John felt that it was the most exciting day of his life.

'It was a massive occasion. I went really early to the racecourse and my older sister, Marie, and I took up our position on a low wall near the winning post at about noon.

'The first race was 2pm and the Derby was the second race. We had to grab our place early or we wouldn't get any view; I don't think we had sandwiches or anything, but we were so excited, hopes were very high.'

Arctic Storm, ridden by Bill Williamson, was drawn on the wide outside of the twenty-four runners, which posed a dilemma: he could either jump away fast, and pull across to a good position, or he could hang back, conserving stamina, and hope to thread his way through the field. As he had won the Guineas over a mile and this was a mile and a half, he chose the latter. The tactics so nearly came off. Halfway through the race, at the top of the hill, the horse suffered interference and almost fell, leaving mud on his knee. But he recovered, and then flew up the straight passing horse after horse. Only the French-trained *Tambourine II* remained in front of him. One stride past the post and *Arctic Storm* was ahead of him, but on the line – where it counted – he was beaten by a short head.

'My father was philosophical,' John recalls. 'It was the most exciting day of his career.'

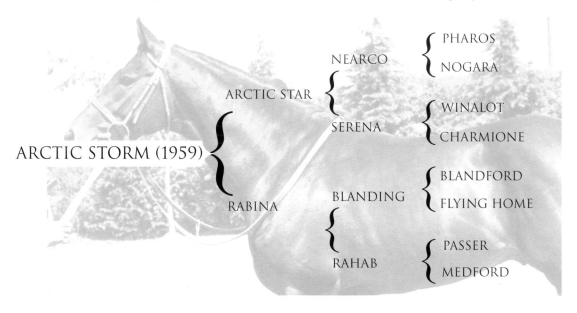

ARCTIC STORM (1959)
- ARCTIC STAR
  - NEARCO
    - PHAROS
    - NOGARA
  - SERENA
    - WINALOT
    - CHARMIONE
- RABINA
  - BLANDING
    - BLANDFORD
    - FLYING HOME
  - RAHAB
    - PASSER
    - MEDFORD

Above: Azurine *is led in after winning a maiden race first time out at Phoenix Park in July 1959, ridden by Jackie Power and led in by lad Ned Doolan. John Oxx senior (centre, in hat) and three friends, l-r Jim McKenna, Jerry Killeen and Eddie Dolan; far right is John Oxx junior just before his ninth birthday. The following year the filly finished third in both the Irish 1,000 Guineas and Irish Oaks for owner Miss E.C.B. (Betty) Laidlaw.*

Below: Chatting, *Paddy Sullivan up, with lad Tommy Forde and John Oxx senior after winning a race at Phoenix Park.*

There had been a huge build up to the day, being the first Irish Hospitals Sweeps-sponsored Derby (of which more later) and suddenly Ireland was playing host to the richest race in the world.

John recalls, 'It was a huge PR stunt and a great boost for Ireland; I remember such excitement and it was very inspiring for a youngster, there was no turning back for me after that.'

As a child John junior rode a bit and played a lot of sport – an all-rounder – and at one time he thought he might ride in some bumpers. But his father, a busy trainer, always needed space for owners'

Nurses make the draw for the Irish Hospitals Sweepstakes in Ballsbridge, circa 1940. The Irish Hospitals Sweepstakes was founded in 1930 to pay for hospitals in Ireland when the young state could not afford to do so itself; in 1962 it sponsored the Irish Derby since when the race has been one of Europe's most important Classics.

horses so didn't want a 'bumper' horse taking up a valuable stable. Instead, young John just rode for fun, putting up poles to jump in the paddock where his house now stands, and riding out on the Curragh, but not competing.

He remembers the 1960s as a golden age in Irish racing. It was the time of Tom Dreaper with his galaxy of supreme stars headed by *Arkle* in the NH sphere, while on the Flat both P.J. Prendergast and Vincent O'Brien sent enough winners over the water to be leading UK trainers. Also, within Ireland there was strength in depth of American owners, many of whom would do a 'grand tour' of Europe culminating in watching their horses winning on the Curragh and elsewhere in Ireland, their horses spread among trainers large and small. It was a time of loyal and steadfast clientele across the board.

JOHN OXX SENIOR

For John Oxx senior it all began before then.

In 1943, during 'the Emergency', he was thirty-three years old and had taken out a licence to train. Since that time the name 'Oxx' has been an integral part of the Irish and international racing scene. Incredibly, in his very first year he trained a Classic winner, *Solferino* in the Irish St Leger.

John Oxx began as a private trainer, firstly to James McVey for four seasons and then to A. T. Adams. His base was a moveable feast his first three years, initially at Summerseat near Clonee, and then in the Phoenix Park, but in 1946 he moved to the Curragh and four years later bought Currabeg, with direct access on to the Curragh. The family business has been there ever since, with both John senior and his son John junior currently working there.

Moving to the Curragh proved fruitful for in his very first season he trained a filly called *Lady Kells* to win the Phoenix Stakes ridden by John (Jackie) Power, who was to be his long-time first jockey. Power is another name synonymous with Irish racing.

Lady Kells began an enduring tradition for the Oxxes, as both father and son gained reputations for winning with fillies – but they have not been without outstanding colts, either.

When John Oxx senior set out on the public trail in 1948, just a year after marrying Maisie Moriarty, he had only nine horses. Soon John and Maisie had two children, Marie and John, and it could have been a nail-biting time, but as the winners rolled in so did the owners and success spiralled. Today, John Oxx junior trains one hundred horses.

Below: Ridgewood Pearl *and Johnny Murtagh win the Breeders Cup at Belmont, USA, for trainer John Oxx in 1995. His owners, the Coughlans, erected a statue of* Ridgewood Pearl *at The Curragh.*

The plus side of John senior's reputation with fillies was the trust he gained with studs who, knowing that John Oxx would run on merit rather than laying a horse out for betting purposes, were more than happy for their fillies to go into training with him.

Ten years after going public, John Oxx headed the leading trainer list based on the amount of prize-money won. Interestingly, this was not a year that he won any valuable Classic race, so it was sheer consistency from his runners that secured the title for him.

He was also leading trainer on a number of races won in 1966 and 1967, in both of which years he won the Irish Oaks, first with *Merry Mate* and the next year with *Pampalina*. By this time he was already an old hand at training Classic winners – after his debut success he won the 1960 Irish Oaks and St Leger with *Lynchris*; the 1962 Irish 2,000 Guineas with *Arctic Storm*; the Irish Oaks the next year with *Hibernia* and, gaining Classic success three years in a row, the 1964 Irish St Leger with *Biscayne*, a total of seven Classics in the 1960s, plus the Champion Stakes at Newmarket in 1962 with *Arctic Storm*.

Arctic Storm was an unlikely Classic winner being by an unraced stallion, *Arctic Star*, out of a mare that cost £35.

Opposite left: Sinndar *and Johnny Murtagh winning the 2000 Derby at Epsom for trainer John Oxx.*
Above: Azamour, *trained by John Oxx, wins the St James's Palace Stakes at Royal Ascot, 2004*
(Michael Kinane, green) from Diamond Green *(on the rails).*

ARCTIC STORM & TOMMY FORDE

Foreign travel was still relatively unusual and for *Arctic Storm*'s lad, Tommy Forde, it was a big day. He was probably typical of the stable staff of the day, 'doing his two', which in his case both happened to be Classic winners, the filly *Lynchris*, and *Arctic Storm*.

Tommy grew up in a thatched cottage with his parents and four sisters in Rathbride, Co. Kildare, about a hundred yards down the road from the entrance to Father Moore's Well. The well is said to have healing properties and was to play a part in Tommy's life; Father Moore's hat went to Tommy after the priest's death and visitors came from all over the country to touch it for healing. Today it is with Tommy's son, Michael, and he still receives visitors. Tommy went to the local primary school in Milltown where the headmaster was strict, but Tommy was able to outwit him. A few apple trees stood near the school playground and when the apples were ripening the headmaster would rotovate and rake the ground around the trees, so any footprints from boys daring to steal apples would show up in the earth. Tommy got around this by wearing boots twice his size and managing to seize a few nice ripe apples without fear of being caught.

About the only horsey connection was that his father was a blacksmith, but at fourteen, Tommy took his first job working with racehorses on the Curragh, where he was fed, clothed and taught to ride. After a spell in Newmarket he took a job on the Carton estate, Dunboyne, where he met his wife, Jenny, at 'one of them dances'. Tragedy followed when she died when their son, Michael, was a baby. It was very hard for a single father to look after a baby alone, and one day, having no other option, Tommy wrapped the baby up and took him to the bog during turf harvest time. A vehicle came along and by sheer chance the driver stopped just short of a 'pile of rags'. The only thing was for Michael to be reared by one of his aunts, but he cried so much when Tommy visited him, cycling from Kildare to Edenderry, that Tommy had to wait until his son was asleep before he could return home.

Below: Trainer John Oxx receives his prize from Queen Elizabeth with owner The Aga Khan (left) after Azamour *won the 2005 King George VI And Queen Elizabeth Diamond Stakes held that year at Newbury while Ascot was closed for refurbishment.*

Urban Sea, *dam of both* Galileo *and* Sea The Stars. *She died in 2009.*

When he was working at John Oxx's, Tommy was nearly a model employee who rarely, if ever, drank of an evening, but there was one time when, most uncharacteristically, he had had a couple of drinks and they left him the worse for wear. He hobbled into work the next morning feeling very sick and begged the head lad to put him on a quiet one. The safest horse in the yard was found for him, but as they were circling at the gallops Tommy fell asleep and tumbled off his mount.

Arriving on the scene, John Oxx asked in dismay, 'What happened to Tommy?'

'Well, sir,' said the head lad, 'didn't she throw a quick buck, she didn't give Tommy a chance.'

'Well,' said John Oxx, 'you can never trust a quiet one.'

Tommy Forde's 'two' were *Lynchris* and *Arctic Storm*, both of them Classic winners, but

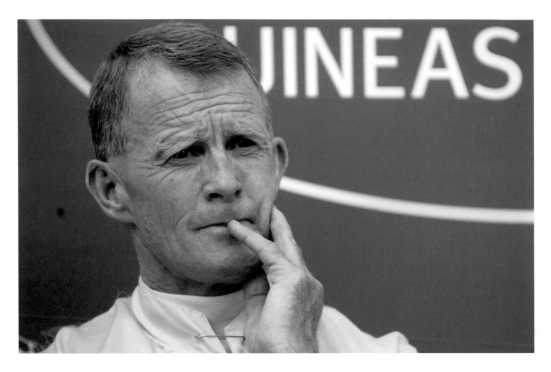

Previous page: Poetry in motion: Sea The Stars *and Mick Kinane win the 2009 Stan James 2,000 Guineas at Newmarket.*

Above: Michael (Mick) Kinane followed his 2009 2,000 Guineas with the Epsom Derby on Sea The Stars *just two weeks before his fiftieth birthday; the previous winter, with such a feat in prospect, he went running five miles a day while also racing in Dubai. His father, Tommy, won the Champion Hurdle at Cheltenham on* Monksfield.

it was *Arctic Storm* who found his way to his heart. Each morning, before cycling from Milltown to Currabeg, he filled his pockets with crab apples, cutting them in half first to prevent the horse from choking. As soon as he went into the stable *Arctic Storm* would smell the goodies and nudge Tommy's pocket. In later years, when *Arctic Storm* retired to stud in Kinnegad, Tommy used to visit him every Sunday on his motor bike, which had by then replaced his bicycle. The horse always whinnied his greeting to him.

When *Arctic Storm* was in training, Tommy used to groom the horse until his coat shone; *Arctic Storm* never looked better or glossier than in his Classic year. He won the Irish 2,000 Guineas, but went under by a head to *Tambourine II* (trained in France by E. Pollet and ridden by Roger Poincelet) in the Irish Derby, sponsored for the first time by the Irish Hospitals Sweepstakes.

The brainchild of one of Ireland's most influential racing supremos, Joe McGrath, the package for 'the richest Derby in the world' was brilliantly publicised and promoted by him and his Sweeps partner, Spencer Freeman.

The Irish Hospital Sweepstakes was founded in 1930 to pay for hospitals in Ireland when the young state could not afford to do so itself; with lotteries illegal in Britain and America, huge numbers of tickets were bought covertly and many millions of pounds were raised.

Its sponsorship of the Irish Derby in 1962 transformed Irish racing, bringing with it a huge purse and thereby drawing the best colts from abroad to contend it. It brought the Irish Derby on to the world stage – more than half a century after another Irishman had tried to do the same.

Richard Eyre 'Boss' Croker was a larger than life Irish American who dominated Democratic Party politics in New York City's Tammany Hall. The child of a family who had fled the Irish famine in 1846, he fought his way from the streets to the halls of power. On his return to Ireland he rebuilt Glencairn beside Leopardstown racecourse and established a stud there, now covered by the British Ambassador's residence.

In *Orby*, trained by James Allen, he had a horse of Classic potential; he set his sights on the Epsom Derby. Support for *Orby* became a *cause célèbre*, which was heightened when a decidedly snooty English press rubbished his chances: 'The turf in Ireland has no spring in it, the climate is too depressing, and no Irish trainer knows enough to even dare to compete for the greatest race in the world,' wrote William Allison in *The Sportsman*.

But *Orby* was special and won the Derby, beating *Wool-winder*, owned by Col. E. W. Baird, one of the Stewards who had banned Croker's horses from being trained in Newmarket. On his return to Ireland, *Orby* was awarded the Freedom of Dublin and Freddie MacCabe, Croker's racing agent, was famously accosted by a Dublin shawlie: 'Thank God and you, sir that we have lived to see a Catholic horse win the Derby!'

Croker offered to fund the Irish Derby to the same value as the Epsom Derby, on condition he be elected to the Turf Club, to no avail. Nevertheless he was determined his star should run in the Irish Derby, against MacCabe's advice who wanted to avoid the 'rock hard' ground.

Boss Croker was adamant: 'The Irish racing public should see their national hero in action on his home ground'. *Orby* duly hacked up at 10/1 on, although the effort lamed him. It was 1907, and it was to be fifty-seven years before the Epsom/Irish Derby double was achieved again.

Founded in 1866, the Irish Derby had never carried sufficient prize money or prestige to tempt connections of Epsom Derby winners to risk their reputations at the Curragh, and with Boss Croker's offer spurned it was left to the Irish Sweeps to change that; its introduction in 1962 revolutionised Irish racing. With £30,000 added by the Irish Hospital Sweepstakes, the Irish Sweeps Derby became the richest race in Europe. From being a provincial consolation classic the Irish Derby was transformed into the most glittering prize this side of the Atlantic.

Arctic Storm had already won the Irish 2,000 Guineas over a mile and when he returned to Newmarket later that year, after his Irish Derby defeat, he was to redeem himself. The Champion Stakes was first run in 1877 and the ten-furlong contest is one of the autumn highlights in Britain – and *Arctic Storm* became the first Irish horse to win it. Vincent O'Brien followed up with *Pieces of Eight* in 1966 and with *Sir Ivor* two years later, while Paddy Mullins' *Hurry Harriet* scored in 1973; *Cairn Rouge* for Michael Cunningham, 1980; and *New Approach* for Jim Bolger, in 2008.

Undaunted by the narrow Irish Derby defeat, Tommy brought over his life savings to put on *Arctic Storm* at Newmarket. He backed him on the tote, and when he went to collect his winnings he was told to go and get a bucket. That night he went out with some other lads and hid his winnings under his pillow. Up until then Tommy lived in a thatched cottage with mud walls. With his bounty he built a new brick house around his old one, and threw the contents of his old house out of the windows. *Arctic Storm's* owner, the wheelchair-bound Mrs. E.M. Carroll from Fethard, Co. Tipperary, gave him the price of a new roof as a present.

Other foreign travel followed, not only to England, but also Paris. Tommy used to go over in a Lambourn CIE horsebox with travelling head lad Noel Reagan; when asked what hotel they were staying in they replied, 'The Lambourn.' Tommy enjoyed betting, but only on Oxx horses; if the yard had forty-two winners in a season, then so would Tommy. In John Oxx's yard (where both John Oxx senior and now John Oxx junior work), every horse does its best to win.

Tommy remembered a new lad arriving from Co. Clare to begin his apprenticeship with John Oxx, taking one look at the Curragh (which stretches across 4,780 acres) and exclaiming, 'Jeekers lads, who owns the big field?'

Tommy died on 14 April 1987, at the age of seventy-two.

JOHN OXX JUNIOR

In 1979 the current John Oxx took over the licence, having been his father's assistant since 1973. That was the year he graduated as a veterinary surgeon from University College, Dublin where he met, and a year later married, Caitriona O'Sullivan. They had three children, Deirdre, who is a speech therapist and married with one son, Ross; Aoife, a teacher; and Ag Science (Equine) student Kevin, who is studying at UCD.

The training got off to a shaky start at first, see-sawing between good and bad years when perhaps 'the virus', the ubiquitous term for any bug, was about, but John's first winner, *Orchestra*, also became his first group winner that same summer, 1979 of thirty Group 1 winners to June 2009. That includes eleven Classic winners (meaning he has now overtaken his father), the latest being the fabulous half brother to *Galileo*, *Sea The Stars*, winner of the 2009 2,000 Guineas, the Epsom Derby, the Eclipse Stakes and the Juddmonte International.

His first really good year was 1986, with a number of winners, and it took off from there.

'It's a pleasure training good horses,' he says, 'but the most important thing is to train for nice people; I'd rather train a lesser horse for a nice person than the other way round

Kevin Oxx, centre, with his father, John and jockey Mick Kinane after Azamour's *2005 'King George' win.*

– but luckily we have had very, very few tricky customers over the years.

'I forget the bad moments, I don't dwell on them, but my first Classic win, in 1987, the year my father died, was a big moment; a three-year-old filly, *Eurobird*, won the Irish St Leger.

'She was owned by Mr and Mrs Gerald Jennings who, nine years earlier, had had the Irish Oaks taken off their filly *Sorbus*. It was very controversial, for minor interference, and was the darkest day, so *Eurobird's* win was some sort of justice.

'It was also a breakthrough. It came at the right time for us and we were sent yearlings belonging to HH the Aga Khan in the autumn of 1988; the business was growing.'

Two years later he won the Irish St Leger again, this time with *Petite Ile*, but it was in 1995 that he achieved arguably his biggest breakthrough with the great *Ridgewood Pearl*. This strapping chestnut mare won an incredible quartet of top races in different countries in 1995: the Irish 1,000 Guineas, the Coronation Stakes at Royal Ascot, the Prix du Moulin at Longchamp, and the Breeders Cup Mile in Belmont, USA. She was truly world class and is remembered permanently in a bronze statue outside the main entrance to the Curragh

John and Caitriona Oxx with their superstar Sea The Stars, *Newmarket 2009.*

racecourse.

Her local owners, the Coughlans, Sean from Kildare and Anne from Naas, had met in London where he had a number of jobs before settling on construction. As a boy he used to go racing on Irish Derby Day by walking to the far side of the Curragh where it was open and free to all. He would peer through the railings, and see the likes of the McGraths and McCalmonts in their finery, and dream his dream of one day owning a horse good enough to be there.

When Sean Coughlan did start owning it was with the filly *Ben's Pearl* and she won the 1988 Irish Cambridgeshire. She retired to stud and produced firstly *Ridgewood Ben* who won the Gladness Stakes and then, returning to the stallion *Indian Ridge*, she foaled the mighty *Ridgewood Pearl*.

John Oxx recalls her as, 'a cracking filly, big and strong, almost masculine, with a deep girth. She was a powerful galloper, as tough as a colt, and a filly apart to look at.

'She was owned by a super couple in the Coughlans.'

Continuing his tradition with fillies, John Oxx won the Irish Oaks for two years running: 1997, *Ebadiyla*, and 1998 *Winona*.

But it was in the new millennium that John Oxx, a quiet, modest man, respected throughout the industry, reaped real rewards. This time it was with a colt, *Sinndar*, belonging to HH Aga Khan. The bay by *Grand Lodge* won the Epsom and Irish Derbys in the year 2000, as well as the Prix de l'Arc de Triomphe, the only horse ever to have recorded this fantastic triple achievement.

'To win the Epsom Derby is every trainer's dream come true,' says John.

10 June 2000, Epsom Derby Day, was the day after John's daughter, Aoife's, twenty-first birthday, so her parents took her with them as a birthday treat. Three horses were ahead of *Sinndar* in the betting, but his claims were solid (he was beaten only once in his career and that was by a head). As the race unfolded, *Sakhee* skipped clear and only *Sinndar*, ridden as always by Johnny Murtagh, could go with him.

Up in the stands, Caitriona Oxx was having difficulty seeing the race because of the number of large hats blocking her view.

'But I could hear them coming and could see the finishing line and I sensed it was him coming.'

Their day was not over yet. After the Press interviews, John, Caitriona and Aoife were escorted to the Royal Box where they were presented to the Queen Mother. It was less than two months before her one hundredth birthday, 'But,' says John, 'she stood the whole time. She was keen to have a chat, was fascinated and left us feeling she really did want to meet us.'

At last they got back to the car, for which luckily they had a driver.

'We must have been sitting in it for fifteen minutes before any of us said a word, we were just so stunned, and full of emotion and disbelief,' John remembers.

A month later, amid much secrecy and subterfuge, Caitriona managed to have a portrait painted of *Sinndar* for John's fiftieth birthday.

Next was the Irish Derby and more emotion. Could they win the race so narrowly denied to John Oxx senior with *Arctic Storm*? The answer was an emphatic nine-length yes!

And so to France for the Arc, the *crème de la crème*.

'We hardly dared hope, we were afraid we'd used up our luck,' says John. 'But Johnny Murtagh was bubbling with confidence; he's a great man for the big occasion.

'It was a perfect day, beautiful weather, we had a winner there the previous day and earlier on the day our sprinter, *Namid*, bolted in for Lady Clague, our longest-established client. *Sinndar* was the icing on the cake.'

Sinndar had become the only horse to achieve Europe's big three.

Since then John's run of success with colts has continued. In 2003 he had another success with a horse that, like *Sinndar*, *Ebadiyla* and *Dalakhani*, was owned by His Highness the Aga Khan – but it wasn't the one he expected. *Dalakhani* was the star three-year-old of that year trained in Chantilly, France, by A. De Royer-Dupre, but the Aga Khan had another horse with John, *Alamshar*. For stud purposes it was considered more important for *Dalakhani's* career to win the Irish Derby.

'But in my report to His Highness after the Epsom Derby I had said we felt *Alamshar* ran a bit green in that race and should improve. I felt he deserved to take his chance in the Irish Derby, and His Highness sportingly agreed.'

The race itself produced one of the great racing duels of that summer with the Aga Khan's two horses having the race to themselves up the straight, battling neck and neck all the way. *Alamshar* won; it was the only time that year that *Dalakhani* was beaten.

'His Highness ran to greet him in, he was as proud as punch. I think he felt Irish that day there were so many cheers,' John remembers. 'He loves it as a sport and a hobby and understands it; he won't run one just for the sake of it.'

The following month *Alamshar* won the King George and Queen Elizabeth Stakes at Royal Ascot, where the three-year-olds take on older horses, in convincing style.

Azamour was a more than worthy successor to *Alamshar* and was a favourite of John's, though it is hard to believe he did not win a Classic. Instead he added the St James's Palace Stakes and the Irish Champion Stakes to the Oxx CV in 2004 and the Prince of Wales

Stakes and another 'King George' to his tally in 2005.

In 2006 *Kastoria*, owned like *Azamour* by the Aga Khan, added another Irish St Leger to the roll of honour.

Many of John Oxx's horses have won awards and titles, but John himself puts a lot back into racing. He was chairman of the Irish National Stud from 1985-90 and of the Irish Racehorse Trainers' Association from 1986-91, and 1993-96, and on the committee from then until 1999.

He has also been a member of the Irish Equine Centre Board, the Irish Horseracing Authority and of the Mallow (Cork) and Punchestown racecourses. He is a member of the Leopardstown committee, and was for many years a board member of RACE, the Racing Academy and Centre of Education and is currently its conscientious chairman.

In 2008 he was honoured with the Irish Racehorse Trainers Association Hall of Fame award, and there have been a number of other awards over the years.

The ever-helpful Caitriona tries to find a space in John's diary for us to speak; he is in Limerick today, will be in Navan on Sunday – where his once-raced *Alandi* steamrollers the mighty *Yeats* in the *Vintage Crop* feature race; midweek he'll fly to Newmarket to walk the course and come the week-end he'll be back there with his runner, *Sea The Stars*, in the 2,000 Guineas.

The manner in which *Sea The Stars*, whose dam, 'Arc'-winner *Urban Sea* died in foaling earlier in 2009, won the 2009 Guineas was mouth-watering. All the talk beforehand centred around *Delegator*, who finished second, and the other Irish runners filled the next three places, all of them at shorter prices than the winner.

Immediately after the race *Sea The Stars* was installed as ante-post favourite for the Derby while connections returned to their Curragh home to celebrate.

John Oxx showed me his superstar, stripped and gleaming in his stable, a few days after his 2,000 Guineas win. His sheer size sets him apart from many flat racers; that and superb limbs and the way he 'stands over the ground'.

'Bet you'd like to face a fence out hunting on him,' John laughs.

The horse also, noticeably, has the loveliest temperament.

Nowhere was this more clearly seen that at Epsom on Derby Day, 6 June 2009.

Many a supposedly calm horse has been shattered by nerves on this day of days: the huge crowds, noise, lengthy preliminaries and above all the atmosphere that transmits itself to horses as well as humans. Many sweat up profusely.

Not *Sea The Stars*. He took it all in his stride with equanimity and poise.

The fear in advance of the race had been due to stamina doubts on his sire's side.

But by the time he had cruised his way to Derby stardom he looked as if he could easily have carried on further. Although the relatively slow early pace could have helped his stamina, so also it saw him fighting for his head for the first couple of furlongs which could have expended too much energy.

But Mick Kinane soon had him settled in fourth place. Down the hill and round Tattenham corner he came without a trace of awkwardness, hugging the inside rail and, hitting the furlong pole, his long stride stretched effortlessly into the lead; there he stayed, beating the first couple of Aidan O'Brien's six runners, for a magnificent victory.

Mick Kinane, just two weeks short of his fiftieth birthday – 'they've let him out of the old people's home for the day', quipped fellow jockeys – confessed that during the winter in Dubai, realising what a prospect he had in him, he had been running five miles a day.

'He has a very high cruising gear and is so quick. When I first saw him I couldn't believe my luck – he's given me a new lease of life.'

John Oxx also realised from an early age that *Sea The Stars* could be a superstar. 'He had magnificent presence and was a beautiful yearling. He did everything right when he was being broken in, he is so intelligent and has never let us down; now he has gone right up to the top of the ladder.'

It was in 1992 that a young science student with a particular interest in the genetics of thoroughbred racehorses and how to improve their health and racing ability spent a summer riding out at John Oxx's. Today she is an award-winning researcher and lecturer at University College, Dublin, where one of her pupils is Kevin Oxx. She remembers her summer riding out as great fun, particularly the banter between the lads and lasses – and for the fact that it is probably the time she has been the slimmest and fittest of her life. She is Emmeline Hill, grand-daughter of Charmian Hill, the owner of Ireland's greatest NH mare, *Dawn Run*.

DAWN RUN – THE GREATEST MARE

A HUSH HUNG OVER AUTEUIL. The stunned silence was almost palpable in the sweltering heat. Somewhere in the background the French commentary kept going, but the Irish contingent and many other supporters of 'The Mare' did not hear it. 'Their' mare had gone into the flight on the far side jointly in the lead, just as she had all the preceding ones, but in all of those she had gained two lengths in the air. This time she did not reappear at all. She lay on the French grass, her neck broken, killed instantly. The living legend was gone, snuffed out. The greatest National Hunt mare of all time, before or since, was dead. No more little *Dawn Runs* to be born in the future.

All too soon the tongues found themselves again; almost all were to blame the mare's owner, to accuse her of greed in running her horse in June when, fresh from her Gold Cup triumph, she should be turned out for her summer holiday, they said – and still say.

It had all been so different two years before, in 1984. Then, hot on the heels of winning the Champion Hurdle and the Irish equivalent, *Dawn Run* had made it an unprecedented three by winning this same French race, the Grande Course de Haies D'Auteuil, their

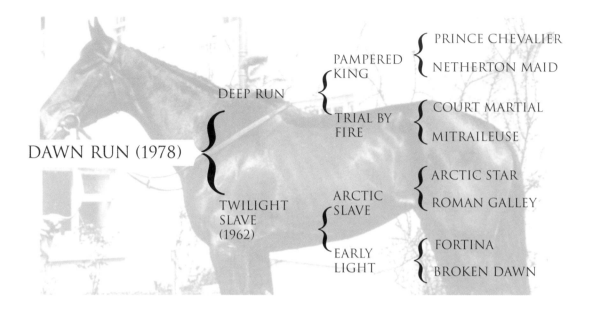

DAWN RUN (1978)

- DEEP RUN
  - PAMPERED KING
    - PRINCE CHEVALIER
    - NETHERTON MAID
  - TRIAL BY FIRE
    - COURT MARTIAL
    - MITRAILEUSE
- TWILIGHT SLAVE (1962)
  - ARCTIC SLAVE
    - ARCTIC STAR
    - ROMAN GALLEY
  - EARLY LIGHT
    - FORTINA
    - BROKEN DAWN

Champion Hurdle. Amid the euphoria and celebrations that followed in the crowded bar, packed and overflowing onto the concourse mostly with fans from across the channel enjoying all the drinks on the owner, she commented in bemusement, 'I never knew I had so many friends.'

I first met Charmian Hill in the early 1970s and enjoyed a memorable day's hunting on one of her horses in west Waterford. Although I didn't buy the point-to-pointer that I'd gone to see, it meant that, a decade later, when Charmian's name cropped up with increasing frequency I began to take note of the mare that was responsible – *Dawn Run* – and to follow her progress.

Charmian began point-to-pointing late in life, at the age of forty, after raising her family, Jeremy, Oliver, Penny and Barton. Early photographs show her racing in a hunting cap, something that has long since been replaced by compulsory crash helmets. She was second in her hunt race to Lord Waterford on her first ride and then beat him in the same race the following year, riding her hunter *Johnny*. She was hooked; rather than being born to it, she had 'acquired' the racing gene. She went on to have several wins – seven of them on the tiny *Boro Nickel* who became her foundation mare – and earned a fearsome reputation.

Diminutive and wiry, she was nevertheless not as strong as she may have been portrayed. There was a day in the eighties that she had a reciprocal day's hunting with me in England; as we were tacking up the two horses I noticed through a crack in the stable wall that the one she was bridling biffed her in the chest; she dropped like a stone into the straw. Without telling her what I'd seen, I quietly popped in and helped her finish the tacking up.

It was on New Year's Day 1974 that Charmian became the first Irishwoman to ride under National Hunt rules and almost inevitably the sobriquet 'Galloping Granny' was coined.

Dawn Run was foaled in April 1978 in Co. Cork by Patrick Mangan, one of whose seven sons, Jimmy, was to train the Grand National winner *Monty's Pass* twenty-five years later. Two days after foaling, the filly foal and her dam, *Twilight Slave*, returned to their owner, John Riordan, who lived near Rathcormack, also in Co. Cork. It was the mare's sixth foal; the third, a colt named *Even Dawn*, went on to win three hurdle races and eighteen chases. The new filly was by *Deep Run* and her development progressed normally for two months, then suddenly disaster beckoned. Her dam's foot became infected, necessitating a bout of stable rest as a consequence of which her milk dried up. Not finding her normal

Below: Eddie and Charmian Hill.

Above: 1986 and Ireland's heroine Dawn Run *(Tony Mullins up) jumps her way to victory in the specially-arranged match with* Buck House.

nourishment, the foal began scouring badly. Her temperature soared to the top of the thermometer, then plummeted to the bottom; the vet did not expect the shivering foal to survive. Had not John Riordan's wife, Prudence, sat up with her night after night, feeding her every three hours from a bottle, the racing world would never have heard of *Dawn Run*. To Prudence, it was only what she would have done for any suffering animal or human.

By the time she was three the filly was broken in for John Riordan by Jonjo Harding from nearby Castletownroche. He found her easier than a half sister *Lek Dawn*, and less impressive as a prospect than her full sister *Twilight Run*. But he had *Dawn Run* looking a picture for the Sales, where he also entered her for the pre-sale show and for which one of the judges was Paddy Mullins; she was placed second.

There was interest enough for her at the sales; she was beautifully bred for chasing, being by *Deep Run*, out of an *Arctic Slave* mare and her half brother *Even Dawn* had already won eighteen races. She looked a grand stamp of horse in the making with no conformation faults and an excellent temperament. Had she been a gelding there is little doubt that she would have fetched an impressive price.

In later years there were various stories of trainers who almost bought her, or who would have done had she been a gelding. But for one prospective owner there was only one fear, that she would make at least £10,000, and for Charmian Hill that was out of her price bracket.

She went along anyway, more in vague hope than keen anticipation.

The bay filly was Lot 29, early in the day of 6 November 1981, at the Ballsbridge Sales in Dublin.

A year earlier, when *Dawn Run* was still roaming the fields in Co. Cork, Charmian Hill had been fighting for her life in a number of hospitals, following a race fall that was fatal to her mount, *Yes Man*. This was a horse she had put in training with Paddy Mullins when she acknowledged he was too much for her at home, and she had won both a bumper and a hurdle race on him. When Paddy suggested it was time to send him chasing she agreed, but asked him who would ride.

'You,' came the reply, 'he goes well for you.'

So well in fact that, after schooling successfully, they won their very first chase together and in the process made Charmian Hill the first woman to ride winners in bumpers, hurdles and steeplechases.

It was in a later hurdle race that *Yes Man* turned a somersault over his tiny rider. He was killed with a broken neck; she was rolled on as if by a steam roller and also suffered a broken neck as well as broken ribs on both sides of her body and kidney injuries. During three long and painful months in various hospitals Charmian vowed to herself that she would race again. But her weight dropped from eight stone to six and a half, and her muscles wasted away. Eventually she tentatively rode her favourite hunter, and from there Paddy Mullins allowed her to ride out on a quiet horse. She bought a replacement horse in *Diamond Do* and amazingly the pair won a bumper soon afterwards. The indomitable galloping granny was back.

Not long after, *Diamond Do* got injured and could not race again, so it was back to looking for a replacement; but without insurance to be collected it was with a limited budget that Charmian set out to Ballsbridge that November day.

Beneath the 'gaunt and unfurnished' frame and gawky schoolgirl stance of Lot 29 was a filly that immediately caught her eye.

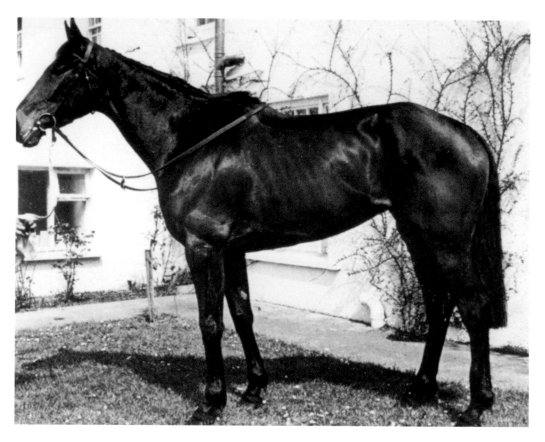

Opposite top: Dawn Run *as a three-year-old.*
Opposite bottom: The tiny Boro Nickel *won seven races and became foundation mare to many winners, seen here with the equally small Mrs Hill in the saddle.*

'She just walked out of the box,' Charmian's voice was still filled with excitement years later. 'I said to myself, "Wow, here we go", I really and truly did.'

Because her finances were limited she had asked her son, Oliver, if, for the first time, he might like to share a horse with her. Oliver, who hadn't gone beyond riding ponies, agreed and left the purchase up to his mother; her total budget was £6,000.

On seeing the filly and liking her so much, Charmian was even more afraid the lot would make too much money – but at 5,800 guineas the hammer dropped and the mare that would make history was going back to Charmian Hill's Waterford home.

Eddie and Charmian Hill had an unpretentious, but lovely, home at Belmont on the outskirts of Waterford where Eddie was a highly respected GP, in some respects ahead of his time; he was a larger-than-life character with an interest in modern art, but very little in horses. The thirty-three acres that surrounded the ranch-style house ran down to the banks of the River Suir, ideal for the horses and for themselves: they stocked their garden with a constant supply of vegetables and soft and hard fruit. One luxury was a swimming pool in which the couple swam before breakfast in the morning, but they were never extravagant. They had met as undergraduates at Trinity College, Dublin, where Charmian was only the second female to read agriculture. In Eddie, Charmian had met her match; they were good foils for each other and excellent sparring partners, both quick-witted, highly intelligent and determined.

When it came to set up home together they cycled from Enniscorthy to Waterford, a distance of some thirty miles, and began married life in a town house from which Charmian cycled two miles each way to tend to her hunter, *Johnny*. With his practice established, the couple eventually moved to their ideal home, Belmont. It was close enough to Waterford City for Eddie's work and near enough to the country for Charmian to recommence her childhood love of hunting, begun when visiting her grandmother at her farm in Monksgrange, Co. Wexford, during the school holidays. As a seven-year-old, she used to ride around on a donkey and, once the family moved there when she was about eleven, she spent every winter day that she could out hunting. Neither her parents nor brother and sister was interested in horses and the young Charmian used to have to force herself to stay awake after a long day's hunting so that she would not be barred from going out again the next day. Eventually she found a mare that she named *Boro Lass* after the local river; she would have been capable of point-to-pointing, but Charmian's parents would not allow it.

Although her parents had no interest, her grandmother, Adela Orpen, had been brought up on the prairies of Kansas, USA. Adela lived with her father and a governess, the rest of the family having died. In order to see above the high prairie grasses, she used to travel everywhere on a pony. Eventually she moved to Ireland when she inherited Monksgrange, the Wexford farm that was to prove so influential to her grand-daughter, Charmian. After Charmian's unmarried brother died in the mid-1980s, Monksgrange passed on to Charmian's eldest son, Jeremy. Of all of Charmian's grandchildren, it was only Jeremy's son, Ben, and daughter, Emmeline, who rode, firstly on *Miss Abba*, an outgrown pony of Henry de Bromhead, now a trainer in Co. Waterford, and then on *Magic*, the pony who got jockey Richard Hughes, son of trainer Dessie, started. Ben runs regular schooling bumpers on the Monksgrange land and also runs Celtic Equine, importing saddlery and other equine goods.

Today, Jeremy and Ben run a few brood mares on Monksgrange, including some of *Boro Nickel's* descendents. In 1996 Ben won first time out on *Boro Bow* in a bumper in Listowel, meaning Jeremy had bred both horse and rider. The mare went on to finish third behind *Istabraq* in the Irish champion novices' hurdle at Punchestown. *Boro Bow* was out of *Boro Quarter* who won the Galway Plate just over a month after *Dawn Run's* death, and *Boro Quarter*, in turn, was out of Charmian Hill's foundation mare, *Boro Nickel*.

Today, *Boro Bee* (by *Bob Back* out of *Boro Bow*) is in training with Tom Mullins and so far has twice finished second in bumpers from four runs.

During the early 1990s Jeremy turned his attention to Flat breeding with almost Classic results. He bought a mare inexpensively who was beautifully bred, but had a crooked leg. She was by *Dancing Brave* out of a full sister to *Shirley Heights*. Jeremy's judgement was that the malformation was as a result of injury and not genetic; she produced four winners from four foals. One was *Miletrian*, by *Marju*, who won the Ribblesdale Stakes at Royal Ascot and the Park Hill Stakes in Doncaster, and she also ran in the Oaks and Irish Oaks. Another, *Mr Combustible*, by *Hernando*, won the Chester Vase, and Newbury's Geoffrey Freer Stakes beating *Millenary*. He was fourth in Galileo's Derby having led for much of the way, and third in the St Leger to *Milan* – not bad for a colt out of a crooked mare.

Above: Early Light *(by* Fortina*) was* Dawn Run's *maternal grand-dam; she won four point-to-points over banks.*

Once home from the Sales, *Dawn Run* proved a paragon for an older rider (Charmian was now past sixty), learning willingly and accepting life with equanimity, so much so that when Charmian felt her mare was ready to go into training with Paddy Mullins, she told him, 'She's so placid that I'm afraid she may never be a racehorse. I don't think she'll be competitive enough.'

That was to change. In her very first race she pinned back her ears when a rival tried to pass her so that Charmian, riding her, thought the mare was going to try and bite her opponent. She finished eighth and then fourth next time, but her third run on 23 June 1982 was a day Charmian would never forget. It began badly when Charmian opened her post at breakfast and to her horror discovered the Turf Club did not intend to renew her licence to ride, due on 1 July.

Charmian protested in no uncertain terms. Why, she wanted to know, when she had bought two horses (*Diamond Do* and *Dawn Run*) to ride herself and had won on both of them, were they refusing her? She supported her appeal with a petition, and among the signatories was Ted Walsh. He called her a 'game woman' and declared she was doing no harm to anybody, causing no interference, and was a lot better than many other amateurs.

But this had no effect on the Turf Club, who replied:

'Your letter of 25 June has been placed before the Stewards. I very much regret having to inform you that the decision as conveyed to you in my letter of 21 June has been confirmed. The Stewards are not prepared to grant you a Permit to ride in INH flat races. Yours sincerely, Michael Keogh, Registrar.'

So the exact reason was never given, but perhaps a clue lies in a supremely polite letter from the same official to Charmian Hill dated 7 November 1977, nearly five years earlier, when her application to ride in races open to professional jockeys was turned down.

Below: 23 June 1982 and Charmian Hill rides Dawn Run *to her first success, a bumper at Tralee; earlier that same day Mrs Hill had heard that the licensing stewards did not intend to renew her riding licence.*

'Thank you for your letter of 1 November. It was with the greatest reluctance that the Stewards declined to grant you permission to ride your own horses in professional NH races.

'Your experience and ability are already a matter of record and don't need to be related here. It is not usual for the Stewards of the Governing Bodies to advance reasons for the withholding or refusal of Licences but your letter in my opinion deserves an answer, and compels me to raise, with the greatest respect, the question of your age.

'You must accept, as fact, that the Stewards would not grant a Licence under INHS Rules to a professional rider of similar age, and to accede to your request would be a contradiction of accepted policy. While I fully understand your particular position, the original decision must stand.'

Charmian greeted the new letter from the Turf Club with fury and was determined to fight it. For starters, she would go out and win on her new mare that very day. *Dawn Run's* previous race had been confined to four-year-old mares only, but this one, at Tralee, was open to mares and geldings, of four and five years old. Four of the ten runners were preferred to her in the betting but in the race only one of her nine rivals got anywhere near her, and *Dawn Run* won by a length. For Charmian Hill it was a timely slap in the face to the licensing stewards; to the general public it was just an ordinary winner of a run-of-the-mill bumper.

In spite of her vociferous pleas and plenty of written support from within the industry, Charmian's licence to ride was not renewed. So *Dawn Run's* first win was Charmian's last. For the mare's next two runs it was to be Paddy Mullins' youngest son, Tom, in the saddle, winning both, and thereafter she became the mount of professionals, notably Tony Mullins and Jonjo O'Neill.

After winning a maiden hurdle in Navan, *Dawn Run* was thrown in at the deep end for a valuable hurdle at the Leopardstown Christmas meeting; her chance was rated virtually nil and Paddy Mullins had another more fancied runner ridden by his elder son, the champion amateur Willie. It was after *Dawn Run* won this that thoughts of Cheltenham could be entertained, but for the mare to enter the big time Charmian felt that a more experienced Irish jockey should be used. It was tough on Tony Mullins who demonstrated time and again that the mare ran for him. (Tony was leading claiming rider in 1982, third in the Irish senior table in 1983 and tied for the title in 1984, the year *Dawn Run* won the Champion Hurdle.) But in 1983, for *Dawn Run's* first visit to the Cheltenham Festival, the ride went to Ron Barry; they finished second in the Sun Alliance Novices Hurdle won by Michael Dickinson's *Sabin du Loir*. His *Badsworth Boy* won the Queen Mother Champion

Chase later that afternoon, but it was the next day that Michael went into the record books by training the first five home in the Cheltenham Gold Cup, headed by *Bregawn*.

Tony Mullins was back in the saddle to win on *Dawn Run* at Liverpool and then the very next day the pair ran a length second to the newly-crowned Champion Hurdler, *Gaye Brief*. Just over two weeks later *Dawn Run* turned out at Punchestown to storm away with the Champion Novices Hurdle, (won in 2009 by Willie Mullins' *Hurricane Fly*).

At the time it was still the intention to send *Dawn Run* chasing the next season (1983-84) history shows that she not only stayed hurdling, but also won the Champion Hurdles of England, Ireland and France; in eight hurdle races that season she won seven and was second in the other. In the first of these at Down Royal and in the last two, at Liverpool and Auteuil, Tony Mullins was aboard, but for Cheltenham and the others Charmian stuck to her policy that the mare should be ridden by a leading jockey and in Jonjo O'Neill Charmian was assured of the very best. For a mare bred for chasing it was an amazing season hurdling.

The next autumn saw *Dawn Run's* keenly-anticipated first run in a steeplechase. Navan was packed that dank November day and the big crowd was not disappointed: *Dawn Run*, ridden confidently by Tony Mullins, was foot perfect. The racing fraternity admired and praised both *Dawn Run* and her owner, as well as her trainer and rider. The Gold Cup beckoned.

But a minor injury ruled that out for 1985 and the mare had the rest of the season off.

When *Dawn Run* returned she had, if anything grown; she was a magnificent stamp of chaser, never more evident than when running in France against little Flat-type horses. Her season did not begin until December, which is late (and significant in view of those who slated her running in June). She won her first two chases in Ireland, but when she went to Cheltenham in January, to give her a dress-rehearsal for the Gold Cup in March, she hit a fence hard on the far side and dislodged Tony. He hung on valiantly to the reins and actually remounted to finish well behind, but after it Jonjo received the call up once more.

The next race was for the Cheltenham Gold Cup, the blue riband of steeplechasing, for which her experience was just four chases, three wins and an unseated rider – barely out of the novice league.

The race produced an epic to rival any in steeplechasing's annals and remains spoken of to this day. *Dawn Run* had led for most of the second circuit, but when she was overtaken by two horses at the last fence she looked beaten: an honourable third was the best to hope for because it is most unusual for a front-runner to re-take the lead once passed. But neither *Dawn Run* nor Jonjo O'Neill was 'usual'. Defeat was not a word in their joint dictionary.

The famous Dawn Run *colours on board* Clifdon Fog *(bred and owned by Charmian's son, Jeremy Hill), led into the winners' enclosure at the 1999 Punchestown festival by Charmian Hill's grandchildren Ben and Emmeline.*

Somehow Jonjo galvanised her to recoup the lost ground and more. In as stirring a finish as has ever been witnessed up that final infamous hill they got up to win on the line.

The whole of Prestbury Park went wild; there was no question of keeping singing and cheering fans out of the unsaddling enclosure and in they poured, delirious in their happiness. She had become the first – and so far only – horse to win both the Champion Hurdle and the Cheltenham Gold Cup.

The wild euphoria affected *Dawn Run*, hyping her up to such an extent that next time out, at Aintree, she was so excitable that she fell at the very first fence.

A famous private match race followed at Punchestown against her old rival, *Buck House*, the Queen Mother Champion Chase winner. With Tony Mullins back in the saddle, she simply stamped her authority, running over a shorter distance more suitable to her rival.

And so to France, and to the start of a dark time for Charmian Hill.

Below: Emmeline Hill with her children, Isla and Henry, in 2008

Dawn Run's death on that fateful, fiercely hot day in Auteuil in June 1986 sent shock waves throughout Ireland; news of it spread as if by smoke signals. In one swipe the racing world turned on the mare's owner, the lady from whom so many had been happy to accept copious drinks on the French track two years earlier. Now they vilified her.

Tragically her husband, Eddie, had died from a stroke the year before, between *Dawn Run's* Champion Hurdle and Gold Cup; Charmian needed his brand of inimitable support more than ever now. Widowed and castigated, her health suffered and three years later, on Christmas Day 1989, Charmian suffered a fatal second stroke, on the very day one of her grand-daughters, Jessica Charmian, was born. Her ashes were scattered to join Eddie's in the family graveyard near Monksgrange, the beautiful Co. Wexford family home that held such happy childhood and lifelong memories for her.

None of Charmian's four children took to riding, but her eldest son, Jeremy, continued breeding from her *Boro* line; two of her ten grandchildren became good riders, Emmeline and Ben. They are two of Jeremy's three children and they both also have pony-mad toddler daughters, Isla and Gabriella. In Emmeline the term 'racing blood' takes on a whole new conception – in a high-powered, intelligent way that would have seen Charmian giving a spirited 'thumbs up'.

A PhD in human genetics with her thesis on understanding the origins of the Irish people, Emmeline was the recipient of a Science Foundation Ireland President of Ireland Young Researcher Award in 2004. Apart from her research work into thoroughbred equine genetics she is also a lecturer in the new Animal Science – Equine course at University College Dublin, where one of her pupils is Kevin Oxx.

Her interest in animal behaviour and evolution began while studying natural sciences at Trinity College Dublin where her professor was Paddy Cunningham, now chief science advisor to the government; he was one of the few people focusing on thoroughbred research. He steered Emmeline away from zoology and towards horse genetics, persuading her to return to Trinity after a spell working in Rome.

'The subject had not been exploited and I could see a future in it,' she says.

It was as recently as 2007 that the equine genome sequence was completed, providing the tools enabling an understanding of genes contributing to equine health, performance and athleticism. Emmeline is concentrating her research on understanding the science of how genes contribute to the function of exercise physiology in thoroughbreds. She believes that, long term, the work may act as a model for understanding muscle strength as well as obesity and diabetes in humans.

'The thoroughbred has been bred selectively for four hundred years for the lean, muscular type and we can now unravel the genes that breeders have been unknowingly targetting. The further aim is to find the DNA differences between the top, elite racehorses and the non-winners, and the differences between sprinters and stayers,' says Emmeline.

'Genetic information can provide an additional tool to breeders; what we have is just part of the tool kit; that doesn't take over from the conformation, environment and breeder's choice, they all play their part.

'But success comes to risk takers, those not afraid to take on new ideas; science is about methodology, logic and fact. I'm very fortunate to work with many in the industry and

particularly with Jim Bolger; he has been interested from the beginning and facilitates our research.

'The summer I had at Oxx's helped me understand how a racing stable works, including the fun and banter between lads.

'I just can't believe how lucky I am to be doing the job I am, I love it.'

And so the racing gene remains in the Hill blood …

Many metaphorical stones have been cast at Charmian Hill, but had *Dawn Run* won on that fateful day in France her fans would have enthusiastically hailed their queen. Since then, other Irish horses have run – and won – in June in Auteuil, a course that is maintained in superb condition.

Her son, Jeremy, is philosophical. 'A horse like *Dawn Run* goes into public ownership and a lot of things are said by people who don't understand the complexities of race-planning involved.'

It is his belief that the mare died before the flight, something he feels is backed up by the video.

Dawn Run herself has become a part of Irish folklore, revered throughout the land. It is not just her wins that she is remembered for, twenty-one from thirty-four runs, including five of her seven chases (she was never beaten in a chase when not a faller), but the manner in which she achieved them. Her sheer courage and determination, her battling qualities and will to win. Her magnificent feats, and especially her Cheltenham Gold Cup, will never be forgotten.

Opposite left: The Match. The reigning Gold Cup winner Dawn Run *and Queen Mother champion* Buck House *appear to be swapping notes.*

3

MULLINS MAGIC

'REVERED' IS NOT TOO STRONG A WORD TO DESCRIBE the esteem in which Paddy Mullins is held. In fifty years of training he was never once in trouble with the stewards and his integrity and good manners have been passed on to his children and grandchildren, who continue the family name both in training and riding.

I paid my first visit to the Mullins home back in 1985 when writing the book, *Dawn Run: The story of a champion racehorse and her remarkable owner* (published by Arthur Barker Ltd). The chapter on the Mullins family is a cameo of the time and I am reproducing it here, with pertinent updates after:

> The Mullins are a remarkable family. If *Dawn Run* had an amateur breeder and amateur owner/rider, she had a true professional in her trainer. There cannot be many families which share the Mullins' record: Paddy, his wife Maureen, and their five children have all ridden winners!
>
> Paddy Mullins was born on 19 January, 1919, the son of William Mullins who farmed

Above: Dawn Run *jumped beautifully and won easily.*

land adjacent to Paddy's present home at Doninga, Gorsebridge, Co. Kilkenny.

Leaving the old Co. Wexford town of New Ross by a drawbridge over the River Nore where it is wide and flat before it joins the River Suir, one heads up a steep, narrow valley of a tributary towards Graiguenamanagh in Co. Kilkenny. The landscape soon becomes a ravine with heather and bracken on the hills and the river winding deeply below. It is rugged and wild and very rough and windy going on towards Gorsebridge where the land flattens into a fertile plain. A little corn grows but it is mostly small fields with large, unclipped hedges on top of stone-faced banks, a few sheep dotted about.

Gorsebridge itself is a fairly typical small Irish town with an unsightly stone quarry and a huge, ugly, castellated decrepit building. It is home of a big feed mill; of well-known horse and pony sales; and of Ireland's leading NH trainer, Paddy Mullins.

Doninga, his home, is a long, low white farmhouse made ever brighter in the dull grey winter months by colourful red and orange berries covering the entrance wall just off the road, barely a mile out of Gorsebridge.

A cheerful fire usually glows at one end of the long, low sitting room which is tidy and tastefully furnished, with comfortable easy chairs. Racing pictures and photographs adorn the walls, including a very happy Maureen winning her one and only race, and some favourite paintings by the artist, Snaffles. A few racing trophies, including some Waterford Crystal, are dotted around and a set of twelve plates with pictures of all the family members winning are on a table.

Almost everywhere one goes in Ireland, Paddy's training is praised and with fifty or so horses, the biggest NH yard in Ireland, his record simply stands for itself. He knows when it is right to run a horse or not.

The main stable yard is right behind the house, with more boxes which were completed early in 1985 to one side.

'I said I wouldn't build any more,' Paddy smiles ruefully, 'but once you start turning owners away, they won't come back.'

The stables built up gradually over the years after Paddy took over the licence from his father in 1953 having been his assistant for thirteen years before that. In only fairly recent times has the stable reached the upper echelons, establishing a high reputation with many winners of big races both on the Flat and jumping.

Paddy grew up with hunting being a natural part of life and he enjoyed following the Kilkenny hounds on a variety of ponies, able to take his own line without fear of barbed wire or electric fencing. He joined the Pony Club, and tried his hand at show-jumping just

Below: Tony Mullins waves to the Paris crowd after Dawn Run *had won the 1984 French Champion Hurdle at Auteuil. Two years later she was to die in the same race.*

as many another kid of his day, until there was a natural progression into the local point-to-points.

He won about twenty-five and was also successful fourteen times under Rules, scoring on the Flat, over hurdles and in chases, all as an amateur.

Breeding, rearing and training all followed on, and he still derives a lot of pleasure from breeding, keeping up to half a dozen mares.

He has always had a mixed yard of jumpers and Flat horses, and he finds it particularly lucrative to sell a good filly for the Flat.

'They are like gold dust,' he says. 'I've sold a few and it all helps.'

In his early years, Paddy could be described as a small-time trainer, and one feels there is a hidden conflict within him preferring it that way, out of the limelight, but yet having the perfectionist's wish to keep on improving.

The only drawback for a man of his nature to the success that the latter brings is the accompanying attentions of the Press.

'I hate publicity,' he says, his chin almost on his chest, his hands grasped tightly round his locked knees. 'They all talk through their pockets!'

Paddy is a non-betting man, and his is a non-gambling stable.

'I've no time for the Press at all,' he suddenly becomes animated. 'I never back my own horses, and only very occasionally have a few pounds on others for interest.'

His reason is simple: 'Because it's nearly impossible to win.'

Nevertheless, his aversion to publicity is unfortunate, because his is a very public profession. 'What the Press

Left: Paddy and Maureen Mullins at home shortly before his retirement in 2005, aged eighty-seven.

Above: Maureen Mullins in the paddock of their local track, Gowran Park in 2007, with some of her grandchildren, l-r Emmet, David and Patrick.

says does worry me a bit,' he says, looking up from under the lock of silvery grey hair falling across one eye. Certainly Paddy is a very sensitive man.

Only when he shows someone the horses in his yard does he unwind a little and start to relax as he is with the animals he loves, none more so than *Dawn Run* who has a box on her own, almost facing the back door of the house. It is very big and light and airy and filled with deep straw.

There are about fifteen lads in the yard, in addition to all four of the Mullins' sons. Of the four, only Tony is professional, because he is the only one who can do a low weight. It was Tony's good fortune, Paddy believes, that William was heavier, because he is probably just as good a jockey, and particularly capable over fences. William point-to-pointed for many years and is an excellent judge of pace.

William is the eldest son, and also the only one to have spent any length of time away from home, having stayed for a valuable period in Australia as assistant trainer to Neville Beg. Now he is assistant trainer to his father.

He went on to make his first ride at the NH Festival at Cheltenham a winning one on *Hazy Dawn* in 1982, and two years later he did it again, winning the four-mile NH Chase on *Macs Friendly*. In the year in between he won the Liverpool Foxhunters on *Áth Cliath* (the Irish word for 'Dublin') as part of the first ever all-Irish combination of horse, owner, trainer and rider to win it.

George is the second son and although another thoroughly capable amateur rider, the farm is his main interest, running both the home farm, where all the training takes place, and Paddy's other farm three miles away. He rides out once every day, then gets on with the farm work while the other brothers ride out at least another two lots. George's riding career may seem a little overshadowed by his brothers, yet he has ridden getting on for twenty winners himself.

Tom is the youngest, and he has the enviable record of being unbeaten on *Dawn Run*. It was he who rode her in her remaining two flat races after Mrs Hill was forced to quit.

The Mullins daughter, Sandra, the eldest of the children, is married to Dublin businessman Peter McCarthy, and she still visits the family home most weekends. It was in 1982 that she had about five rides on the Flat, winning the Rose of Tralee ladies' race and finishing third in a one-off invitation charity race, the Ceville Lodge Stakes, for trainers' wives and daughters at local Gowran Park.

This was the race won by her mother Maureen on her only ride on a professional racecourse and she did it in style, too, storming clear on *Razzo Forte* to win by six lengths. It need not have been such a surprise because as Miss Doran before she was married, Maureen was an able point-to-point rider.

Third son Tony's career almost ended the day it began. In 1979, at the age of seventeen, he had his first ride in a point-to-point on a horse called *Creidim*. It was the local Kilkenny Hunt meeting, held on the inside of Gowran Park racecourse. Tony, who by all

Left: Willie Mullins
Opposite right: Tom Mullins

accounts had been a bit of a devil-may-care in the Pony Club, was helpless in what happened, for the horse died in mid-air and landed heavily on top of his slim young rider. Tony's leg was so badly broken that he was unable to ride again for over a year.

Yet by 1982 he was leading claiming rider (the equivalent of an apprentice on the Flat), and in 1983, his first as a senior jockey, he finished third in the jockeys' table to Frank Berry. One year later he tied for the title, having at one time been five winners clear of Frank Berry. The mishap on Tony's debut only made him more determined than ever and, as I write, he has yet to have another really serious injury.

Besides Tony and his amateur brothers, the yard has Peter Kavanagh as second jockey and several of the lads have 'boys' licences.

The rides seem to be sorted out amicably between the brothers with no arch-rivalry, probably because Paddy holds the reins and they all respect his judgement.

For a mother, to have a racing son can be a nerve-wracking experience; to have all four riding regularly might be a nightmare. Maureen is very much a part of the business set-up, as well as looking after the home and family. She is a most able and efficient secretary, one of the things that keeps her busiest is the almost constant ringing of the telephone.

Paddy says, 'When the boys were growing up, I never dreamt that they would all ride. But they don't want to do anything else and so we have to live with it, although people think we're daft!'

The sons have all had strictly equal opportunities, and the horses have certainly turned out well for them. To maintain a degree of independence, all four indulge in a little buying and selling in their own right. 'The horses have been good to us,' Paddy says warmly. 'I wouldn't wish for any other life.'

Above: Tony Mullins

One of the best mares he ever trained was *Height O'Fashion*, remembered for some epic struggles against *Arkle*, running him to a neck once when receiving three stone of weight. (When they first met four years before in a handicap hurdle, she had to give him 23lbs.) She was also second to him in the Irish Grand National. These races came after she had left Paddy who never raced her against the great horse, but he did win twelve races with her, including the Irish Cesarewich.

Paddy lets a training programme evolve round a given horse without hard and fast advance plans. But of one thing he is sure. He will never run *Dawn Run* in the Grand National.

In fact he had never had a runner in the Grand National until 1985, when Tony Mullins led for some way on *Dudie*. He trained *Nicholas Silver* earlier in the same season that he won, and he had formerly trained *Andy Pandy* who set up a long lead before falling in the big race.

'Either I haven't had the right horses or the owner hasn't wanted it,' he says without a tinge of regret. This is a man who has a soft spot for his charges.

'I let the horse tell me what it is capable of. My aim is to do the best I can with them.'

Most of the galloping is done in the fields around Doninga and, as with most Irish trainers, much of the schooling is done either on the Curragh or after racing on courses. Indeed, some racecourses occasionally stage an all-schooling day, split into sessions over different distances.

And so it was on 31 July 1982, with the ground hard and Mrs Hill having failed in her bid to have her licence renewed, that eighteen-year-old Tom Mullins teamed up with *Dawn Run* for her final bumpers at Galway.'

Nearly a quarter of a century has slipped by since that piece was penned. Whereas in the mid-80s Paddy had the country's biggest stable with fifty horses, several now top one hundred, including Paddy's son Willie Mullins, with his all-conquering team of talent, primarily in NH. Other, mostly Flat stables, also house a hundred or so, like John Oxx, Dermot Weld, Aidan O'Brien, and Jim Bolger and the chiefly NH/mixed yards of Noel Meade and Jessie Harrington.

In the intervening years since *Dawn Run*, one of the biggest highlights in Paddy's career, and certainly the most warmly welcomed, was his training in 2003 of a Classic winner, the Irish Oaks.

On 13 July that year *Vintage Tipple* lined up on the Curragh against ten rivals; her starting price was 12-1, for all that Frankie Dettori was in the saddle. Paddy's was a non-betting stable and, in spite of her long price, connections were hopeful; she had won both her starts as a two-year-old for new owner, Pat O'Donovan; he had paid only 16,000 guineas for the filly bred by Sir Edmund Loder of historic Eyrefield Lodge on the Curragh.

Vintage Tipple, by *Entrepreneur*, had finished second on her outing prior to the Irish Oaks but in this, the most important day of her life, she put 1½ lengths between herself and her nearest pursuer, *L'Ancresse*.

The scenes that followed were more like an Irish winner at the Cheltenham NH Festival than the staid and smart Classic Flat scene; both codes were united in greeting Paddy, aged eighty-four, and his heroine.

Interestingly, Paddy rates his 1973 Newmarket Champion Stakes winner, *Hurry Harriet*, the best he ever trained, better than either *Dawn Run* or *Vintage Tipple*. 'She had the class,' he says quietly, and describes how impressive she was on the gallops with Sandra in the saddle.

Among Paddy's outstanding qualities were his patience and his empathy with horses. There was a time, many years ago, when a 'rogue' horse gripped him on his shoulder in the stable. Instead of pulling back or shouting, or struggling to free himself, Paddy didn't react, he just stood there talking to the horse who still had its teeth embedded on his shoulder (luckily he was wearing thick jackets); he remained like this for about two hours until eventually the horse gave up and let go of him.

Paddy was an expert at finding the psychological key to his horses; his children could occasionally be found running safely between the legs of 'dodgy' ones, and sometimes the clue was to give a particular horse a different lad; personalities count with horses as with people, and given the right carer a horse's racecourse performances would improve.

TRAINING SONS

Three of the Mullins sons, Willie, Tony and Tom, are well-established trainers themselves, all with many winners, while George has a reputable racehorse transport business. Sandra also joined the training ranks in 'a small way'. Three of Paddy's grandsons are now jockeys or amateur riders. George's Emmet often rides under NH Rules for his uncles; Willie's son Patrick has been leading amateur rider for the last two seasons, and Tony's son, Danny, is a leading Flat apprentice to Jim Bolger, already in the top twenty of the senior professionals list.

As a trainer, Tom Mullins' most memorable stable star was probably the gutsy little mare, *Asian Maze*, who was also Paddy's last winner before his retirement in February 2005, aged eighty-seven. *Asian Maze*, a chestnut owned and bred by Mrs C.A. Moore, was a 2½-mile specialist who won nine races, four of them at Grade One level. She won the hearts of many in her trail-blazing feats.

Perhaps her greatest moment – and a particularly fond memory for Tom – was when she defeated reigning dual champion hurdler *Hardy Eustace* by seventeen lengths in the 2m 5f Aintree Hurdle in 2006. The young trainer trusted his instincts and it was a memorable

Below: Tony's son Danny with Celestial Island *after winning at Galway in 2008.*

victory, one that proved, indisputably, that he was his own man. For good measure, she ran again at Punchestown over three miles and won that, too.

Although *Asian Maze's* career began with Paddy Mullins, the bulk of it was under Tom's training. She provided a kick start and he would be the first to admit to his luck, but since then he has continued to prove himself, not least with *Chelsea Harbour*. So far *Chelsea Harbour* has won seven races over fences and hurdles, and was second, ridden by Tom's nephew Emmet, in the Thyestes Chase in Gowran Park. The pair was well fancied for the 2009 Aintree Grand National, the horse having finished ninth in the previous year's race, with Davy Russell in the saddle – but unfortunately they fell at the third.

Among the horses Tony Mullins has trained is *Barrow Drive* who contested the country's leading chases, a most consistent horse who ran fifty-five times. A Grade 1 winner, he scored thirteen wins in all. Tony notched a Cheltenham Festival winner in 2007 with *Pedrobob*, who won the Vincent O'Brien County Hurdle for owner Barry Connell. He was ridden by Philip Carberry on that day to score from a field of twenty-eight. In all, *Pedrobob* won seven hurdles and one of two chases.

Many of Willie's current top horses are discussed in chapter nine, which looks at Ruby Walsh, the high-class jockey who has ridden so many of them to victory. Suffice to say no matter what and how much the success, Willie remains charming, unruffled, polite – and sociable. The yard and office run like clockwork. The climax of 2009 was the stuff dreams are made of: three winners at Cheltenham and an amazing twelve at Punchestown.

The television pundits were understandably full of praise.

Robert Hall said, 'I can't praise Willie enough, so many [horses] don't come back from Cheltenham but his do. He has five or six of the best horses in the country in his yard.'

Discussing the clash between *Mikael D'Haguenet* and *Cousin Vinny* running in the same race, it was because, 'Willie couldn't split them working at home.'

Tracy Piggott also commented on how well his horses had come out of Cheltenham; *Cousin Vinny* had been working 'out of his skin all week, they had to take each other on.'

They are class individuals, and the intention is that both will go chasing next season from the start. 'They can come back to hurdling if it doesn't work.'

Willie said, 'I have a great team at home, they deal with day to day matters; we have good owners who keep bringing nice horses into our yard.'

Part of the success was down to there being no coughing or other virus in the yard; the horses were really healthy which helped it all go so well.

Ted Walsh reminded viewers that Willie was a fine rider himself, and has a good back up in his wife, Jackie. 'He appreciates all and doesn't take anything for granted.'

As the yard grows and smart new office, stables, wing to house are added, so nothing is spoilt in any way. There is a good atmosphere in the yard that permeates from the boss downwards.

Of Willie's favourites of former years, the Aintree specialist and Grand National winner *Hedgehunter* is one, while the evergreen *Florida Pearl*, an outstanding chaser, is another. The winner of six of his first seven starts (he fell in the other), *Florida Pearl* won the Hennessy Cognac Gold Cup at Leopardstown's February meeting in 1999, 2000 and 2001 and then, after being unplaced for two years and suffering niggling setbacks, he put up a superb performance to win it a fourth time in 2004. This was also a training feat of the highest order in what turned out to be *Florida Pearl*'s last run. Apart from making this 'his' race, *Florida Pearl* during his career also won the 'King George' at Kempton Park, beating *Best Mate* in 2001, and the Royal and Sun Alliance Novices Chase at Cheltenham in 1998; and the 1997 Champion Bumper there; he ran in both the Queen Mother and the Gold Cup, finishing second to *Looks Like Trouble* in the latter; he ended with a career total of seventeen wins from thirty-four starts, exactly 50 per cent.

THE NEXT GENERATION

In few families has the racing gene been passed down more strongly than with the Mullins: Danny son of Tony, Emmet son of George and Patrick son of Willie are emerging stars already riding high in the galaxy.

Danny Mullins, son of Tony and Mags Mullins (she is a trainer on her own account), showed a precocious talent from a very young age. Less than five years after winning the 12.2hh Pony Jumping Championship at Dublin for a second time he was riding in his first Classic on the Curragh.

Danny was show-jumping at the RDS in Dublin, twice winning the 12.2hh pony Jumping Championships in 2003 and 2004, and then winning pony races – 126 of them – before being allowed, at the tender age of fifteen, to sign up as an apprentice to Jim Bolger, the numerous Classics-winning trainer with the added talent of bringing on young jockeys as well as horses. Over the years he has nurtured champion apprentices who have gone on to be top senior jockeys like Willie Supple, Seamus Heffernan and Kevin Manning, (who also became his son-in-law). A number of top jump jockeys have begun their careers under Jim Bolger including Dean Gallagher, Paul Carberry and the NH jockey who has put a whole new slant on records, Tony McCoy. And another protégé? No less than ace trainer Aidan O'Brien himself.

Within two weeks of passing his sixteenth birthday, Danny was given his first ride, and less than a week after that he scored his first win, on only his second ride, making all the running on *My Girl Sophie* over 7 furlongs at Leopardstown; his parents' gamble was paying off.

Within days of that first win Danny had doubled his score to two in a big handicap during Guineas weekend at the Curragh; from there his burgeoning career swiftly snowballed. His first 'outside' win came for his uncle, Tom, with *Reload*, and later in the season he won a major handicap at Leopardstown with the same horse. Also that summer he won three races at the 2008 Galway Festival, aged just sixteen.

Danny relaxes his horses down at the start, as was seen to great effect at the 2009 Guineas meeting where he rode in his first Classic, the 1,000 Guineas. He went down to the start early on *Duaisbhanna*, one of three Bolger runners, and could be seen keeping her quietly on her own while the remainder circled. They jumped off to a good start, before fading in the race won by *Again* with one of Jim Bolger's third, *Oh Goodness Me*.

Bucking the family trend of NH racing and amateur riding, there is every prospect that Danny Mullins will become a top professional Flat jockey. As I write, although still a claimer, he lies at seventeen in the top twenty professional flat jockeys table.

He recorded perhaps his finest achievement to date when landing the €140,000 Tote Galway Mile European Breeders Fund Handicap with Rock and Roll Kid, trained by his father. 'This is the best moment of my life,' declared Tony Mullins in the winner's enclosure. 'To win a feature race at Galway is very, very special and for my son to ride it makes it even more memorable.'

In the early summer of 2009 Jim Bolger told me, 'Danny is a very talented young rider with a bright future. He is a credit to his parents.'

George's son Emmet Mullins often rides for his uncle, Willie; he began riding, and winning, as an amateur for a couple of seasons and turned professional at eighteen. Only a short while later, he broke his shoulder and had two months recuperating; losing rides through injury is a blow at any time, but especially when trying to get going in the paid ranks.

He is not a Mullins for nothing, however, and in April 2009 he scored his twentieth win of the season in style when steering *The Midnight Club* to victory in a novice hurdle at the Punchestown NH Festival. The pair looked out of contention turning into the straight, but Emmet brought *The Midnight Club* with a brilliantly-timed run. It was his third win in four rides on the horse and brought his career tally to over thirty.

His ride in the Aintree Grand National (which ended at the third) made him the third Mullins to have ridden in the race, following in the footsteps of Willie and Tony.

It is hard to believe that it was as recently as December 2005 that Patrick Mullins (son of Willie and Jackie) rode in his first race, as a sixteen-year-old schoolboy. His first win came the following June on *Diego Garcia* and the pair won again at Tralee in August. The race was the prestigious Havasnack flat race that Willie had contested twenty times without scoring. However, his brother Tom did win it in 1982 with none other than *Dawn Run*.

Three and a half short years after his first ride, Patrick Mullins was breaking records. At Kilbeggan in April 2009, he steered *Borrowaddy* to victory in a handicap hurdle to notch his forty-eighth winning ride of the season; in doing so he broke Ted Walsh's thirty-three-year-old record for the number of winners ridden by an amateur in one season. The horse had failed at odds-on on its previous run, but Patrick appeared full of confidence as he ranged up to join *The Bay Lad* jumping the second-last. He still sat motionless approaching the final obstacle then sent his mount on to score with plenty to spare. Afterwards Patrick told the Press, 'I'm delighted to break Ted's record, but if he had been riding the horses I have been riding he would probably have ridden sixty or seventy winners!'

Before the season was out Patrick had topped half a century, taking the amateur title for the second year. Earlier in the season Nina Carberry had been about fifteen clear of him,

Opposite: The incomparable Paddy Mullins.

but strength in depth saw it out for Patrick, a charming young man with typical Mullins' manners. Both he and Nina do their respective families proud.

The strength came not only from his father's stable, but also from the saddle. About half way through the season Willie quietly admitted that Patrick had become a very strong rider, able to punch a powered finish. Patrick, for all his six foot plus frame, also tucks himself into a neat position – and, like Nina, he also has a 'racing brain'.

Cousin Vinny is his outstanding ride and although officially unseated at the last at Leopardstown, the horse was so nearly on the ground when he stumbled that it was far from simply 'falling off'. Patrick has been on board for all nine of the horse's runs, and they have won five of them. The partnership is incredibly exciting for the future.

It was in February 2005, shortly after his eighty-seventh birthday, that Paddy Mullins retired. The decision was not easy and the family was divided on the correct course: two in favour, two against, one not sure. In addition, a member of the Turf Club itself had been down to see him to ask him not to retire.

But, always a perfectionist, he became worried that he should do something wrong, such as maybe forgetting to take a horse's passport racing one day and being fined for it, or otherwise finding himself in front of the stewards, something that had never happened to him personally throughout his career, though he had had to appear on behalf of jockeys from time to time. He called time.

Two short months later, greeting his eldest son home from winning the Aintree Grand National with *Hedgehunter*, it was apparent that Paddy had made the right decision. He looked younger and more relaxed; the worry had gone.

January 2009 brought a great family occasion again when Paddy Mullins celebrated his ninetieth birthday, Maureen at his side, his children and grandchildren all around him.

FIVE GENERATIONS –
THE INCREDIBLE HARTYS

AINTREE GRAND NATIONAL 1969; Dubai World Cup 2009. The Harty family epitomises Ireland's long tradition of involvement in horse-racing. The sport is so much in the Hartys' blood that five generations have ridden in Listowel.

It began with brothers Michael and Ned Harty who in the 1880s both rode winners at the Kerry track. Michael's son Cyril Harty was an amateur, while his four brothers, Michael, Henry, George and John were all professional jockeys. This enthusiasm and skill extended down to the next generation, as Cyril saw one son – Eddie – win the Grand National on *Highland Wedding*; another son, Buster (Cyril), was an amateur rider of note. Buster's daughter Sabrina is a successful trainer and Eddie's son Eddie took up training late, yet won a race at the Cheltenham Festival on his first visit across the water with, appropriately, a horse named after his grandfather, *Captain Cee Bee*. Eddie senior's younger son Eoin trains in California and in 2009 won the world's richest race with *Well Armed* in the Dubai World Cup. Eddie junior's son, Patrick, at sixteen has begun racing too, including a ride in Listowel, and is an enthusiastic recruit to the amateur riding ranks.

Above: The Harty family, front, left to right: Herbert, Anne (who married Guy St John Williams), Ealonar (who married Pat Hughes), John. Seated, l-r: Paula, Una, Buster; standing: Eddie.

The family originated in Co. Limerick where some branches remain. Delma Harty, twin daughter of Henry Harty of Patrickswell, took over her father's stable and trained *Khan* to win the 1970 County Hurdle, becoming the first woman to train a Cheltenham Festival winner; *Khan* was ridden by Lord Petersham (who later became Lord Harrington, and died in spring 2009). Delma went on to become Ireland's first female steward when appointed to the old Limerick racecourse panel. Her brother, Henry (Harry), rode many wartime winners and later became a Turf Club official.

EDDIE HARTY, FATHER & SON

Like father, like son. Eddie Harty senior and Eddie Harty junior look physically different – one short and jockey-like the other tall and lean – but the trait that binds them is their focus; once they have put their minds to something they go out and give it their best shot.

This resulted in Eddie senior representing Ireland in the 1960 Rome Olympics competing in only his third ever horse trials (he had previously been a top show jumper); and in Eddie junior training a Cheltenham Festival winner only four years after obtaining his licence at the age of forty-two, having been previously (of all things) a banker!

Eddie junior has some abiding, if somewhat vague, memories of childhood. He was seven when his father won the Grand National on *Highland Wedding* and his Aunt Anne (married to Guy Williams) was baby-sitting.

'I remember tracing the course in the black form book as the racecourse progressed, and of him being mistakenly called a faller, and then Anne going berserk when he won.

'I remember visiting Toby Balding's stables the next day to welcome the heroes home; and of Dad's celebrity status when he brought the trophy along to my primary school at Baydon, Wiltshire.'

The next year it was disappointment; Eddie was on a school trip to Belgium when he heard that the partnership had finished 'only' fourth in the great race.

All ready to go – for the 1960 Rome Olympics, l-r mounted: Capt Harry Freeman-Jackson, on St Finbar, *Capt Ian Dudgeon (*Charleville*), Tony Cameron (*Sonnet*), Eddie Harty (*Harlequin*), Maj Eddie Boylan (*Corrigneagh*).*

He also remembers his father beating the great *Bula* on a horse called *I'm Happy* at Newbury; of being on the wide sloping lawn at Chepstow and seeing his father's mount, *Nimble Joe*, somersaulting when clear two fences out; and of the interminable exercises his father had to do whenever he was recovering from injury.

Probably his earliest memory of all was listening to the radio as his father rode a four-timer on St Stephen's/Boxing Day, and coming from last to first on *Ranmore* for Fred Winter. But the worst memory is of crying because his father had pulled up a circuit too soon in the Scottish National on *Stalbridge Colonist*.

When his father had the fall that finished his career – he was lucky not to lose his arm – the family left behind their sojourn in England and settled once more in Ireland, where they had in any case spent most of their summer holidays and where Eddie senior had been steadily building up a bloodstock business, sourcing chasers for Fred Winter, Toby Balding, David Gandolpho and Michael Scudamore. The new home was Strawhall on the Curragh and so Eddie went to Newbridge for his secondary schooling.

He never actually had formal riding lessons, he had only hacked occasionally through Lambourn Woodlands, or ridden friends' ponies in Ireland in the summer.

'Dad would be gone to work at Toby Balding's at the crack of dawn and was unable to

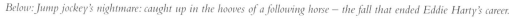
Below: Jump jockey's nightmare: caught up in the hooves of a following horse – the fall that ended Eddie Harty's career.

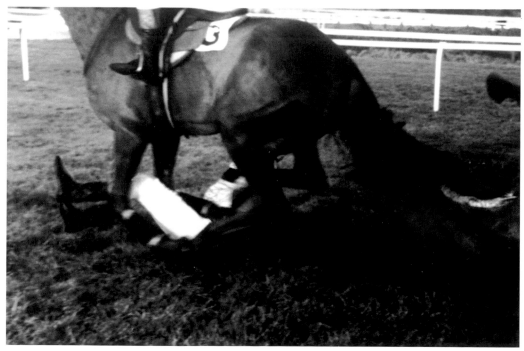

give lessons, but I found riding totally natural. I was given a pony when we moved back to Ireland but I wasn't very interested and didn't like show-jumping, all I wanted was to gallop.'

He then had a black 12.2 pony that would 'run away with the twelve apostles', and gave him a couple of concussions, but he was hooked by the thrill. Next came a white pony belonging to Pat Taaffe's brother-in-law Bill Lyons, outgrown by his children. On *Lucky*, Eddie would have his 'feet up under his chin', which didn't go down too well with the Pony Club.

'I think I was riding about two holes longer than Andy Turnell and rode a whirlwind finish in a hunter trial one day, but I was told "that's not a proper Pony Club seat". That finished me.'

A picture of the occasion, however, shows that his hands were in a perfect position.

Eddie went on to ride in a few bumpers and wanted to be an apprentice jockey.

'I weighed six stone wet through, but then I grew too tall. But I was placed a number of times.'

Once his dream of becoming a jockey was behind him, in spite of – or because of – his upbringing, Eddie initially spurned working with horses. He became the first member of the family to attend college (in Galway, which he loved) where he read English and economics and from there he went to America, home of his grandmother Winifred Smith from a stockbroking family in New York, a place he not only loved, but that also set him on his original career path as a currency trader.

'I wanted to be assistant trainer to my father, but we're so alike in personality we would be bound to clash, so when a currency trading job came up in Dublin I took it and was able to ride out as well.

'One day a vet came into the yard called Marie Cole – ten months later I married her. I always meant to train one day, but with a mortgage and two children I kept putting it off, I felt lucky to have a job. Then in 1996 the bank I worked for was bought by Anglo Irish; we bought the land here at Pollardstown in 2001.'

Planning permission was difficult to get unless he could show he had a business planned, so he went on the Racing Academy and Centre of Education (RACE) course for trainers where one of the other students was ace retired jockey Adrian Maguire.

It inspired him to have a cut at training – and readily accepts this was only possible due to Marie being a partner in Anglesey Lodge Veterinary Clinic.

Eddie coerced some of his bank colleagues to become owners and so the embryo stable sent out its first runners in 2004. From five inmates, four won and the other failed to reach the racecourse.

Meanwhile Eddie senior had a nice foal by *Germany* out grazing on the land; the bay gelding, named *Captain Cee Bee* after Eddie's father Captain Cyril Harty, was broken at three in 2004 and from the start Eddie junior could see his potential and 'minded' him, several times going to a race-meeting, but leaving him in the box if he deemed the ground not suitable. Once the ground came good the horse won a bumper beating *Big Zeb*, but he was 'cast' (stuck when rolling) in his stable before the Championship bumper at Punchestown in April and was unable to run.

So it was a break and then on to Killarney where his nine-length victory caught the eye of legendary owner J.P. McManus who promptly bought him. J.P.'s policy is to keep the horse with its current trainer, where possible, so *Captain Cee Bee* remained with Eddie – who now had his sights set firmly on Cheltenham in March. But three times before then he failed to run because of the ground so that by the time he travelled across the water the Anglo Irish Bank Supreme Novices Hurdle was his first run for four months. He was also Eddie's first runner in England – sponsored by the very bank he had left four years earlier.

So *Captain Cee Bee,* spotted by Eddie senior as a foal and named after his father, stormed up that final hill for a famous victory, getting Eddie junior's training career off to a dream start.

Today, he also has a Listed-winning flat racehorse, *Baron De'L* who has won six races at the Curragh.

CAPTAIN CYRIL HARTY

Eddie Junior's grandfather, Captain Cyril Harty won the last running of the Governor General's Cup for serving officers at Punchestown. He was a founder member of the Irish show-jumping team with Jed Dwyer and Dan Corry while serving on the Curragh. He won the first show-jumping competition for Ireland as a Free State; he was also on the first Aga Khan winning team for the blue riband of international show-jumping competitions at Dublin Horse Show.

As father of eleven children he took up training to supplement his army pay from stables in Phoenix Park; he also began a bloodstock business buying stock for top trainers in England and all over the world.

This rubbed off on his sons Eddie and Buster, and Eddie recalls, 'I was always very focused even as a child and I just had to have horses; I hunted from seven years old with the harriers in Limerick where the family originally came from. I travelled down by train

Above: One Seven Seven, *owned by Sir Michael Sobell, trained by Fred Winter, winning at Stratford with* Eddie *in the saddle.*

Above: Well under age, Eddie Harty won the open pony show-jumping championships (open to all heights) on a 13.2 called Rossa *at the RDS, Dublin when he was just ten years old, showing the style, flair and 'hands' that were to serve him well as a professional jockey.*

and rode whatever I was put up on, then it was show-jumping.'

He won the open pony show-jumping championships (open to all heights) on a 13.2 called *Rossa* in Dublin when he was just ten years old. Clearly Eddie had exceptional talent, with the requisite temperament, beautiful 'hands', and competitive spirit – for all equestrian disciplines.

He went to the Jesuit School in Belvedere, Dublin, and today a picture of him winning the Grand National hangs alongside other old boys such as Archbishop Dermot Ryan and newspaper magnate and racehorse owner Tony O'Reilly.

'But I didn't pay as much attention to my schooling as I did to my horses.'

By the time he was fourteen years old he had ridden in his first hurdle race, and at sixteen he won a three-mile amateur handicap chase at Newton Abbot on *Flaming Dome* for trainer Earl Jones. It was 5 September 1953, his first of many wins under Rules.

By 1960 everything looked rosy – Eddie was newly-wed to Pat O'Neill, and the Olympic Games in Rome beckoned. To qualify for Rome, Eddie rode in just one one-day event and one two-day event; that was his sum total of eventing experience before the Olympic Games.

With several weeks of training with his fellow team members, Capt Harry Freeman Jackson, Ian Dudgeon, Tony Cameron and reserve Eddie Boylan there was no time for a honeymoon and so Rome doubled up as that, too.

His horse *Harlequin* was barely 15.1hh, so small that there were those who put the combination's prospect of getting round the cross-country course at zero. His brother Buster feared he would be killed. But the little horse was agile and jumped superbly, scoring the only Irish double clear round, being faultless across country and in the show-jumping. Having been lying seventieth after dressage, he pulled up to ninth place overall and says, 'The other team members were great, but amateur, and had they been more focused I'm sure we would have finished with a team bronze medal – or even gold.'

Of course, all entrants to the Olympics are amateurs, strictly speaking, but Eddie may have felt that they weren't able to be as committed to riding as he was.

On his return to Ireland Eddie realised that to be able to afford a life with horses it was time to turn professional and be paid to ride the best. And the place with the opportunities was England. Eddie began his professional racing career with former champion jockey

Below: At Sandown debutante Into View *(Eddie Harty) beat established stars* Makaldar *(David Mould) and* Salmon Spray *(Johnny Haine).*

Above: Eddie Harty junior, with his father, Eddie Harty senior
Below: Well done! Eddie Harty senior congratulates jockey Fran Berry after his 2007 Curragh win with Baron De'L
for trainer Edward (Eddie junior) Harty, pictured here with his wife, vet Marie.

turned trainer Tim Molony, originally also from Limerick and then established in Leicestershire, and then moved to Alec Kilpatrick at Collingbourne Ducis in Wiltshire. Among his highlights was winning the Mackeson Gold Cup at Cheltenham on *Jupiter Boy* for Fred Rimell. Another was riding a particular horse making its racing debut for Fred Winter, one that Eddie had not sat on at home first. It was a level weight contest at Sandown and the pair won, beating no less than Johnny Haine on *Salmon Spray* and David Mould on *Makaldar*. The horse was *Into View*, who not surprisingly turned into a star himself; he started joint-favourite for *L'Escargot's* 1971 Cheltenham Gold Cup, in which he finished fourth; he was more at home over 2½ miles, especially at Sandown where he won the Stones Ginger Wine Chase 'a couple of times'.

It was in 1969 that trainer Toby Balding suddenly found himself looking for a Grand National jockey for *Highland Wedding*, his stable jockey, Owen McNally, having been injured a few months before. When he chose Eddie Harty it was the beginning of a lifelong friendship that continues today and, after that famous victory, it was Eddie who became stable jockey and the family moved into the Wiltshire village of Baydon.

Today Eddie, a sprightly septuagenarian, forty-nine years married and a devout Catholic who is not afraid to voice strong views, still rides; he enjoys accompanying his grand-daughter on a Connemara pony called *Freddie* and 'working it in' for her at shows.

He says, 'The University of Life has been good to me and I enjoy mixing with all.'

Of his life in the saddle he adds, 'I am remembered for winning the Grand National on *Highland Wedding*, but I feel my personal highlight as a horseman was in Rome.'

MORE BROTHERS – JOHN AND BUSTER

There was another brother, John, who according to Buster 'may have been the best of the lot.' A qualified barrister and successful businessmen, John competed in the Badminton three-day-event, and rode in the 1964 Olympic Games before emulating his middle brother, Eddie, by becoming a successful professional NH jockey, winning three of Ireland's most prestigious steeplechases.

In 1969 he won the Leopardstown Chase on Major W. A. J. Lockhart's *Gypsando*, trained by his father, Captain Cyril. He followed this up three years later in 1972 by winning the Galway Plate on Mr. J. F. Clifton's *Persian Lark* (by the Derby winner *Larkspur*), and trained by J. F. Maxwell. He capped his career in 1980, twenty-seven years after riding his first winner, (*Springfield Lad* in Clonmel,) when he won the Irish Grand National, no less, on

Daletta, trained by his brother-in-law, Guy Williams, the noted racing historian and writer.

John also acted as honorary treasurer to the Irish Professional Jockeys Association, was chairman of the IRIS; set up a pension fund through their riding fees for retired jockeys, and was a NH liaison officer. Sadly, John died from motor neurone disease in the 1990s. Another brother, Herbert, never raced, but loved hunting and was Master of the South County Dublin Harriers.

At seventy-five, the eldest of the brothers, Cyril 'Buster' Harty, still rides, and can be found harrowing the gallops late into a summer evening before coming inside to cook some supper. His philosophy, needless to say, is to 'keep going'. Until a couple of years ago he would get up on and sort out horses that were 'giving trouble to the lads'.

His daughter, Sabrina, to whom he is assistant, is a competent trainer in her own right, including among her string the tiny but talented *Won In The Dark*, who finished third in

Below: Captain Cee Bee *(nearside) looks less well off at the last flight of the 2008 Anglo Irish Bank Supreme Novices Hurdle at the Cheltenham Festival but he storms to victory over* Binocular *(A.P. McCoy), both horses owned by J.P. McManus.*

the 2008 Triumph Hurdle at Cheltenham, and won the champion four-year-old hurdle at Punchestown.

With a minimum weight of 11.7, Buster became an amateur rider of note, and was attached to the Worcestershire stable of the great Fred Rimell, trainer of four Grand National winners. Buster twice rode the winner of one of England's most famous point-to-points, the Lady Dudley Cup. In 1954 he won a division on Stan Ireland's *Blenalad* and the following year on *Creeola II*, belonging to a farmer, Charlie Nixon, a neighbour of Fred Rimell. *Creeola* was bought for £75 at a fair by Buster's father, Captain C.B., and sold the same night for £200 to Charlie Nixon. A hard puller, *Creeola* was not in the thoroughbred stud book but, Buster remembers, he 'could gallop and win; he was a great big, strong horse who went on to win fifteen races including the Welsh National.'

Buster himself rode winners on all of England's premier tracks, and beat Lester Piggott by half a length in a hurdle race at the long since defunct Birmingham track.

He also won at Cheltenham for *Golden Miller's* former jockey, Jerry Wilson when he was near the end of his training career. Buster also rode in California, now the home of his godson, his nephew Eoin.

Buster always had a good eye for a horse and brokered some memorable deals, including on the show-jumping circuit. He bought *Snowboard* in California who went on to win a Gold Medal in Tokyo; he was also responsible for finding *Grasshopper*, which went to America, but probably the best was *St Lupus*.

'I was commissioned to buy "the country's best horse". I went to a property where I saw a horse that was walked out and he was really good looking; he was very big, about 17hh with excellent conformation. I have very rarely seen a good jumper without excellent conformation.'

The horse was *St Lupus*, a thoroughbred, who jumped fourteen rounds in Dublin without once knocking a fence.

Buster also remembered sorting out a horse called *Gypsando* that was proving very difficult for its owner's daughter, Caroline Lockhart; the horse would throw itself to the ground with her. Buster won a mile flat race with him, and two hurdle races at Dundalk and Gowran Park, but the moment he went back to the girl to show-jump he reverted to his old ways.

Like the rest of the Harty family, Buster had a way with horses – he seems to have passed his skills down to his newly-married daughter, Sabrina, and he is 'so proud' of her now.

Eddie Harty senior has seen his son Eddie train a winner at the National Hunt Festival at

Cheltenham at his first attempt in 2008, and in 2009 his second son, California-based Eoin, trained the winner of the world's richest race, the Dubai World Cup – a marvellous achievement.

EOIN

Eoin has lived 'across the pond' since he was a teenager. He completed the National Stud course in Kildare under the highly regarded eye of stud manager Michael Osborne, a qualified vet who became one of the world's finest stud designers including in Kentucky and in Ireland. Osborne was responsible for twinning Kildare with Lexington, was chairman of Goffs Sales, and a former chairman of the Curragh Racecourse committee and Senior Steward of the Irish Turf Club. He was a member of Horse Racing Ireland and chairman of the Irish Horse Board. As he was also chief executive of Dubai World Racing the victory of his former pupil in the Dubai World Cup would have given extra pleasure. Sadly Michael Osborne died in December 2005, prompting many heartfelt tributes from within the racing and breeding industry.

When Eoin graduated in 1981 Michael Osborne found him a job in Kentucky but after a visit to California he was lured by the temptation of the wonderful climate. Thanks to a contact of his father and Toby Balding he found himself ensconced in the sunshine state – and has never regretted the move, for all that it is a long, long flight to visit home.

The sun shines, the climate is temperate, and he can drive half an hour east to ski in the mountains, or half an hour west to swim in the Pacific – sometimes enjoying both in the same day.

He began in California under legendary Bob Baffert who progressed from training American Quarter horses to becoming the leading US thoroughbred trainer four times and came within a nose of winning the Belmont Stakes, third leg of the elusive Triple Crown with *Real Quiet*. His *Silver Charm* and *War Emblem* also won the first two legs, the Kentucky Derby and the Preakness Stakes.

So by the time he set up on his own, Eoin Harty knew what it took to have either a Classic or Breeders Cup horse in his adoptive country. Before long he had runners in both; in 2001 his horses filled the first two places in the Breeders Cup Fillies Classic for two-year-olds on dirt with *Tempera*, and was second with *Imperial Gesture*.

Two of his stars are *Colonel John* and *Well Armed*, both by *Tiznow* and owned and bred by WinStar Farms. *Well Armed* began his racing career in England and won on his eighth attempt, landing a maiden event on the all-weather at Lingfield in November 2005. Three runs in Dubai, winning on the first as a three-year-old, saw him then move to

Above: 'Rookie' trainer Eddie Harty junior wins with his first runner at the Cheltenham Festival – and here's the trophy.

California where he consistently won and placed, earning a tilt at the 2008 Dubai World Cup in which he finished third.

Colonel John also kept up the good work and won three of his five starts including the Santa Anita Derby before heading for the 2008 Kentucky Derby, but a poor start saw him unable to recover sufficiently and he came home sixth.

The stable-mates were both entered for the 2008 Group 1 Breeders' Cup Classic, with *Well Armed* also entered for the Breeders' Cup Dirt Mile. This was the year that a Pro-Ride surface was used for the first time, which made travelling over more tempting for the Europeans. One of the traditions is the public draw, which that year was held in Santa Anita a week before the big event that has become an annual pilgrimage, in whatever part of America it is held, for thousands of British and Irish racegoers.

Before the draw, Eoin Harty told the assembled press that, '*Colonel John* is an easy horse to keep fit, it's just a matter of whether he is good enough. It's a very deep field this year, everybody has to be respected. There are an awful lot of Group I winners coming over [from Europe]. I think they will adapt to this surface just fine.'

The speedy *Well Armed* was one of the few horses with a victory over the Pro-Ride having won in September by a length under Aaron Gryder, but on the big day, in the Breeders Cup Mile, he never travelled well on the outside and was unplaced, the only time he has been out of the first four since being trained in America.

In March 2009 *Colonel John*, favourite for the million dollar Santa Anita Handicap, ran a temperature on the morning of the race and had to be scratched. But *Well Armed's* all-the-way fourteen-length win in Dubai, where he and Aaron Gryder drew further and further ahead, was ample compensation – and was no fluke.

Although some reports spurned him as a mere handicapper, others were fulsome in their praise, writing that he 'upheld the reputation of the Dubai World Cup with an outstanding performance … the race seemed to lack a true top-level performer beforehand but after his jaw-dropping fourteen-length success the Eoin Harty-trained six-year-old is certainly entitled to be rated up with some of the best World Cup winners according to *Racing Post* ratings.'

A justifiably proud Eddie told the press, 'Eoin rang us after the race and I told him that his horse had looked the best, travelled the best and ran a hell of a race.'

No wonder Eddie and Pat brought out the champagne at their Kildare home after the win! There is hardly a strand of the racing world that the Harty family does not encompass.

THE WORLD OF THE WELDS

CHARLIE WELD

ANOTHER TRAINER WHO HAS MADE THE WORLD his oyster is Dermot Weld, long known as the Master of Rosewell House, close to the Curragh.

His father Charlie Weld grew up at Somerton, in Prosperous near Naas; Charlie's brother, John, the youngest of six, and now in his eighties, still lives there.

John recalls, 'Charlie was always the horse-mad one.'

John was nine years younger than Charlie, and Charlie would always have him as the one to back the horses he was breaking.

'I was small and light so I was always the first up – and the first off, sometimes I was bucked off several times in a day.'

Ironically the serious fall that left him feared dead as a fifteen year-old was not the horse's fault. He was hacking along the road when a dog ran out, spooking the horse.

'He dropped me on the road, but there were no fancy crash helmets then, and I was pronounced dead, loaded on to the back of a lorry, and driven back to my mother, Marie.

'She could see I wasn't dead but I was unconscious for two and a half days, and it affected my balance so I never rode again except for my children's pony, *Dolly*, who lived for nearly thirty years with us.'

Nevertheless, John was an enthusiastic supporter of Charlie's burgeoning riding career.

There was a time when the brothers wanted to run the mare, *Gold Bounty*, bred by their father Bury and mother Marie in the Bishopscourt Cup, which in those days was the hunters' chase for farmers at Punchestown; but they weren't allowed to, because the mare was thoroughbred, which was against the rules then.

Gold Bounty was bred on the farm in 1923 and won many point-to-points; she was by *Goldcourt* (the sire of *Golden Miller*), out of *Knight's Bounty*.

They had another racehorse during the Second World War, a chestnut mare who was half sister to *Gold Bounty*. Because of petrol rationing she was hitched to the cart, took the family to Naas, ran second in her race, and then was re-harnessed to pull them home again. She was sold to England and won about seven races.

Another good mare was *Gallerio*, bred at Somerton and trained by Charlie, who won a number of races both Flat and NH. Her owner was Matt Donnelly who owned the Anchor Hotel on O'Connell Street, Dublin. He was a huge backer and one day he persuaded John Weld to place £500 on her for him, with Paddy Power at even money. The Welds sold another successful horse to Matt called *Copper Jack*; it won first time out in Thurles ridden by Joe Malone, who had been Charlie's head lad.

Another for the Welds, which ran in Mrs Donnelly's name, was *Farney Fox* by *Arkle's* sire, *Archive*. He was bought in north county Dublin and trained by Charlie Weld; he did so well that Charlie went back and bought the mother and bred from her. *Farney Fox* won a couple of bumpers then, ridden by W. Berg, the five-year-old won the 1960 Irish Lincolnshire over a mile at 6-1 in a field of twenty-five runners. The versatile chestnut gelding was also second in the 1963 Champion Hurdle at Cheltenham to the one-eyed *Winning Fair*, ridden by competent amateur Alan Lillingstone. *Farney Fox* also came fourth in the 1963 Washington International.

Another horse bred on the farm and trained by Charlie was *Highfield Lad*, who won the 1959 Galway Plate, and was second the following year; he also won the Mullingar Gold Cup when there was still a racecourse in the Westmeath town.

Charlie met Gita in Naas and they married in Co. Tipperary, then the couple moved to

England, where their only child, Dermot, was born; Charlie was a private trainer to a doctor and continued to ride winners. When he returned to Ireland he rented a place in Castleknock and began training in Phoenix Park, but when Rosewell House came up for sale he bought it, since when it has become synonymous with the name of Weld and the world of racing.

Charlie is remembered as a larger-than-life character who would enter anyone's house with a big, booming voice – and be just as likely to sit down at the piano and play whatever tune anyone wanted, by ear; he never read a note of music.

One of the last memories of him from a niece is of him riding round the yard at Somerton on her orange moped.

DERMOT WELD & ROSEWELL HOUSE

Rosewell House was built by fifteen-times champion Irish Flat jockey Morny Wing after he retired in 1949; he named it after one of his record-breaking six Irish Derby winners. He also won a record twenty-three Irish Classics; he trained from Rosewell and died in 1965.

His neighbours, the Bell family, were related to his wife, Josephine. Two of the Bell sons,

Opposite left: A delightful Weld family photograph showing Dermot Weld as a young boy with two old English sheepdogs, horse Listen In, *his mother behind him and, r-l, his father Charlie and grandfather Bury.*

Ger and Sean, have been Curragh blacksmiths for thirty-six years; Ger works principally for Dessie Hughes, while Kevin Prendergast is the main client for Sean. Between them, over the years, they have shod numerous Classic, Royal Ascot and Cheltenham Festival winners. Their father, Paddy, rode a winner on the Curragh aged thirteen or fourteen when apprenticed to his father Richard. Richard's father, also Richard – the great-grandfather of Ger and Sean – trained the first ever winner of the Galway Plate, *Absentee*, in 1869; he was ridden by another son, William, brother of Richard junior. There were only four races the day of the inaugural prestigious Galway Plate (it was worth 100 sovereigns that year) but nevertheless there was a crowd of some 40,000.

Paddy Bell's brother (Ger and Sean's uncle) Kevin himself trained a Galway Plate winner, *Bunclody Tiger*, in 1974 and also the 1969 Irish Grand National winner *Sweet Dreams*.

Charlie Weld bought Rosewell House after Wing's death and trained horses there for nearly a decade. John Weld remembers that Charlie, who trained nearly a thousand winners in his time, was slowing down in his training operations before retiring in the early 1970s, but that when Dermot took over in 1972 the place immediately began to fly again. Dermot trained an incredible eighty winners from forty-five horses in his first season, aged twenty-three; he has never looked back since.

'I'm right proud of everything he's achieved,' says his uncle, John.

One 'lad' who started with Charlie Weld was Michael Hourigan, the top class mainly NH trainer from Limerick, famous for leading chasers *Dorans Pride* and ten times Grade 1 winner *Beef Or Salmon*. He remembers his spell of life with the Welds fondly and with gratitude. Michael left school as soon as he could, in the June that he was fourteen, and that August signed up as an apprentice to Charlie Weld. Michael is only 5'5" tall and during the five years he was there he rode nine winners.

He recalls, 'They were the best days of my life. It was hard work but fabulous, and like all lads I was always hoping for a ride. Mrs Weld was absolutely fantastic.'

Gita Weld – mother of Dermot and wife of Charlie – is a highly-respected member of the Irish Turf. In 2009, in her nineties, she was still a regular attendee at The Curragh, several times watching her own runners.

It was hard to imagine a win giving her son, Dermot, greater pleasure than to land the 2004 Irish Derby with *Grey Swallow*, a colt bred by his mother. But then along came *Nightime*. On an even more special day in 2006 Mrs Weld's filly won the Irish 1,000

Guineas. *Nightime*'s only run as a two-year-old had come in the race run in memory of Gita's late husband every autumn, the Group 3 C.L. Weld Park Stakes for two-year-old fillies, run over seven furlongs at the Curragh since moving from Phoenix Park, and sponsored by Dermot. He has won it four times: in 1987 with *Trusted Partner, Asema* in 1992; *Token Gesture* in 1996 and with *Theoretically* in 1999. *Nightime* was unplaced, but won her maiden at Cork the following April, prior to her Irish Guineas win.

Dermot says, 'My mother bred as well as owned her, and she also happened to be my twentieth European Classic winner. We had a good celebration dinner that night!'

Of *Grey Swallow*, Dermot says, 'He is definitely one of my favourites of all time, because he was very, very brave, with an engine, and also especially with my mother's connection. He was a wonderful horse. He was champion two-year-old as well as winning the Irish Derby.'

Grey Swallow won his maiden on his debut at Dermot's favourite track of Galway and in all he won six of his fifteen starts, including one when he moved to the USA as a four-year-old. From there he was shipped on to Australia to stand at stud for his new owners.

Instantly recognisable anywhere in the sport, Dermot Weld is a world ambassador for Irish racing – and closer to home, he's the undisputed king of Galway with an incredible record at the now week-long summer Festival. He has won just about every title and every big race in Ireland and, more than that, he has conquered many international races.

A qualified vet, Dermot Weld had a great time riding as an amateur, picking and choosing rides according to his work commitments – and, he admits, to the chance of winning. He had an average one in three strike rate and there was a time when he rode five consecutive winners at five meetings. It was in the vintage days of Bunny Cox, Billy McLernon, Connie Vaughan and other younger ones like Ted Walsh and Barry Brogan.

He recalls, 'I could think I was riding a waiting race and yet Bunny Cox would still do me on the line. You don't see tactics like that today though I think Nina Carberry is an outstanding amateur.'

During his own amateur career he was several times invited abroad and won South Africa's special invitation international race, the one-off Freight Services Champion Hurdle near Pietersmaritzburg. He drew a horse called *Poplin* from Aubrey Roberts' yard for the occasion. This, and the horse drawn by John Lawrence (now Lord Oaksey), who finished third, were joint favourites in the twelve runner field. The whole occasion, organised by Henry Grattan-Bellew, was 'great craic', and included a visit to a game reserve for the

Right: Mrs Marie Weld, Dermot's grandmother, greets Gold Bounty, *an early Weld success, in the 1940s.*

guests.

Dermot Weld's love of Galway began as a boy when, aged eleven, he accompanied his father Charlie, whose home-bred runner *Highfield Lad* won the Galway Plate in 1959. Luck played a part in Dermot's own first success there, as an amateur rider. The champion amateur, Tony Cameron, swapped from Charlie Weld's runner, *Ticonderoga*, to another and Dermot, aged just fifteen, took the ride on *Ticonderoga* to win.

'It was only my second ride; the first had been in Ballinrobe a couple of weeks before, but the horse won, at 100-7. I went on to win that amateur handicap another three times,' he recalls.

He also won the Moët & Chandon 'amateurs Derby' at Epsom, a couple of races in France, and one in America where he was working as a vet in Camden and riding out in the mornings. He persuaded the trainer to let him ride in a race and promptly won.

Of his overseas successes as a trainer, he says, 'It's a question of business, really. I try to place horses to the best of their ability, to maximise their records and then be able to sell them well. In America we have won on the west coast, the east coast, and the mid west. We've won the American Derby in Chicago three times and we're the only non-American stable to have won a leg of America's Triple Crown, the Belmont Stakes, with *Go And Go*, ridden by Mick Kinane in 1990. He beat the favourite, *Unbridled*, by seven lengths.

'And we've done well with fillies over there, *Demitrova* won the Californian Oaks, and *Dressed To Thrill*, bred at Moyglare, won the Matriarch Stakes, both were Group 1 races. I bought *Go And Go* as a two-year-old and he also won in Laurel Park, Maryland, and the

Below: Charlie Weld winning the Kildare Hunt Farmers' race at Twomilehouse in 1946 on the consistent Gold Bounty.

Above: Mary Weld receives the Carling Gold Cup from Noelle Halpin, wife of Tony Halpin (Beamish & Crawford) (right) after the Dermot Weld-trained West China *won the 1988 Carling Gold Cup EBF Handicap of IR£20,000, the feature race of the Festival of Kerry Meeting. Also included are Elaine Ryan, the Cork Rose, and jockey Mick Kinane.*

Futurity on dirt.

'*Pine Dance*, one of my American Derby winners, was a lovely-looking horse, he won that on grass and then was vanned, as the Americans say, to the Pennsylvania Derby on dirt in Philadelphia Park, a $300,000 race that he also won.'

And then there is Galway. From a limited number of National Hunt horses Dermot Weld has won the Galway Plate four times and the Galway Hurdle three times. The tiny *Ansar* is close to his heart. Only 15.2hh, he won the Galway Hurdle and, even more commendably, the Galway Plate twice. For one of *Ansar's* runs in it Dermot arranged for Ruby Walsh to school him at Noel Meade's because he 'didn't want Ruby to walk into the Galway paddock and think he's too small.'

Having sat on him Ruby discovered *Ansar* had springs in his heels, reminiscent of the great show-jumper *Dundrum*, who was also tiny.

Dermot Weld was born on 29 July 1948. He first took out a licence to train in 1972, when he was only twenty-three. That was also the year he married his wife, Mary, and was champion amateur rider for the third time. He's been heavily involved in the world of racing ever since, and today his two sons, Mark and Kris, play their part in the business.

Dermot Weld has won the trainers' title many times; in August 2000 he recorded his 2,578th winner in Ireland to become the country's winning-most trainer, surpassing the record of Senator J.J. (Jim) Parkinson that had stood for more than half a century since 1947.

The previous record-holder, Senator Parkinson was a colossus of Irish racing for half a century. In the mid-1920s he urged that racing should be funded by an off-course betting tax as a means to prop up the sport's finances, which was much needed. For example, in 1928 The Curragh showed a loss on nineteen of its twenty days and on the twentieth, Derby Day, it made a profit of just £15. Jim Parkinson became a record-breaking owner on number of winners in 1907 with twenty-three, beating the fourteen of Lord Waterford's that had stood since 1853. He then beat his own record in 1915 with thirty and in 1926 with thirty-two; his career total prize-money, from 1893 to 1947 amounted to £88,206, beating the approximate £38,000 of the Hon. Thomas Connolly accrued between 1760 and 1796.

Additionally Senator Parkinson broke the trainers' record number of wins in a season in 1901 with 33; 1904, 44 and 1915, 53. In 1939 he was crowned champion trainer for the twenty-fourth time, and by the end of his career in 1947 he had amassed the record for a trainer of £247,814, a record that stood until Tom Dreaper's retirement in 1971 (£289,342).

The Senator's grandson, racing historian Tony Sweeney, produced a massive volume entitled *The Sweeney Guide to the Irish Turf*, which is an invaluable record of five hundred years of racing in Ireland from 1501-2001. Tony's grandfather, great-grandfather William Brophy, and great-great-grandfather Pat Keary all owned the winners of the Irish Derby: Pat Keary in 1870 (*Billy Pitt*), William Brophy in 1880 (*King Of The Bees*) and Jim Parkinson 1917 (*First Flier*); in addition, Pat Keary, an early bookmaker, won the Irish Grand National with *Controller* in the same year as *Billy Pitt*'s Derby.

The story came down the family, however, that Pat believed his best horse to be neither of these two, but a horse called *Bellman* who defeated a famous English mare, *Caller Ou*, when she came to the Curragh. This was no mean feat as *Caller Ou* won forty-nine races from ninety-eight runs including the 1861 English St Leger.

There have been many successful Irish trainers down through the years, but Dermot Weld's record is incredible, by any standards. By 2001 Dermot Weld had amassed £13,690,748 and 2,709 winners, and by February he had topped 3,500 winners internationally.

Dermot remains the only Northern Hemisphere trainer to have won the Melbourne Cup (twice, with *Vintage Crop* in 1993 and *Media Puzzle* in 2002). He was also the first European-based trainer to win a race in Hong Kong, landing the 1991 Invitation Bowl

Hong Kong Mile with *Additional Risk*. He also won the Grade 1 Belmont Stakes with *Go And Go* in 1990, the only European trainer to have won a leg of America's Classic Triple Crown. He has kept the international momentum going with *Dress to Thrill's* win in the Grade 1 Matriarch Stakes at Hollywood Park, and the Secretariat Stakes at Arlington in 2002.

Dermot Weld has trained winners of all of Ireland's Classics. Over the jumps, he saddled *Perris Valley* to win the 1988 Irish Grand National. He has also trained a Cheltenham Festival winner, *Rare Holiday* (Triumph Hurdle) in addition to his numerous Galway, and other, victories. There is one seven furlong two-year-old maiden race in Galway that he has won nineteen times! He was also crowned leading trainer of the Galway Festival for the twenty-fifth time in 2009. But for many people, *Ansar* was his Galway star.

Small, neat, athletic and beautifully bred by *Kahyasi*, *Ansar* had to the end of the 2008 season run in sixty-three races, and his twelve wins have been distributed four each on the Flat, over hurdles and in steeplechases. No fewer than seven, more than half his total, have come at Galway, and again under each sphere. *Ansar* has won on the Flat and over hurdles, including the prestigious Galway Hurdle, but he has an incredible record in the Galway Plate, the country's premier summer jumping handicap. To watch Mrs Kay Devlin's tiny steeplechaser skip his way round Galway, glued to the inside rail, was always sheer pleasure. Even at twelve years old, in 2008, he still finished third in the event. In July 2009, just before the Galway Festival, the gallant *Ansar's* retirement was announced.

Betting does not play a large part in Dermot's life, though he is aware that many owners like to have a punt.

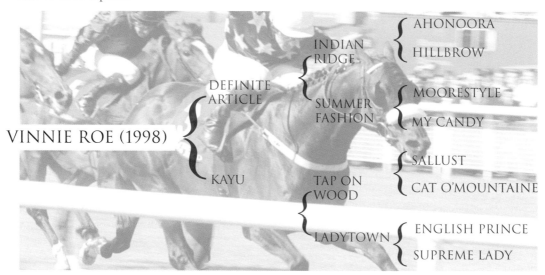

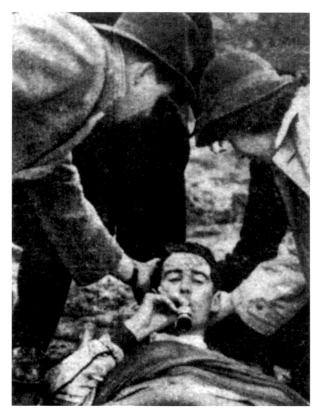

'Winning is what I am interested in,' he says.

✦ ✦ ✦

JIM SHERIDAN & VINNIE ROE

There is one Flat horse of Dermot Weld's that became a particular favourite with the general racing public. Traditionally, it is National Hunt horses which attract the greatest following because of their longevity, as well as their heroics over fences.

Vinnie Roe bucked that trend.

The most consistent and gutsy of horses, he won prize-money in all twenty-nine races he contested spanning six years – and in all bar one of them he was ridden by Pat Smullen. The record four-times winner of the Irish St Leger actually finished out of the frame (first four) three times, but in those, the Irish Derby, the Prix de l'Arc de Triomphe and his second Melbourne Cup, prize-money was distributed down the line.

Vinnie Roe is about much more than records, he was beloved. Dermot Weld's head lad Tom Gallagher, said of him,

'He was my favourite horse, a head man's dream; he was never a problem in all the years we had him. He would let you know if there was something wrong but that was very, very rare, he was such a professional horse.

'He was also very kind. He would get a bit uptight in the stalls at the start of a race, but that was the adrenalin flowing.

'He was a gift of a horse to be around, a beautiful mover; he was the ideal model, not very big, but streamlined.'

Tom, the father of jockey Dean Gallagher, winner of the Champion Hurdle and two French Grand Nationals, has never ridden himself.

He says, 'The boys who rode *Vinnie* always said he rode like a big horse.'

Tom unashamedly loved him more than any other horse and that includes great horses like *Noblesse* and Irish Derby and 'King George'-winner *Meadow Court* both of which he looked after during his time as a groom to 'Darkie' Prendergast.

After Darkie Prendergast died Tom worked for a while for his son, Kevin Prendergast, and then spent ten years as travelling head lad for Jim Bolger, 'a great man to work for'. It was only because of the forty-mile journey each way to work and back, in addition to the driving to the races, that when the opportunity arose, Tom was persuaded to take on the same role for Dermot Weld, five minutes away from his home. Within a short while he became head lad and, now sixty-six, he 'has no intention of retiring, I'd prefer to die – I'd miss the buzz if I retired. You have to be active to survive.'

Opposite left: Charlie and Gita Weld come to the aid of compatriot Aubrey Brabazon who has fallen in the 1947 Grand National (won by the Irish-trained Caughoo *at 100-1). The Brabazons are another enduring family in Irish racing. Below: Dermot Weld trained the 2004 Irish Derby winner* Grey Swallow, *bred by his mother, Mrs Gita Weld.*

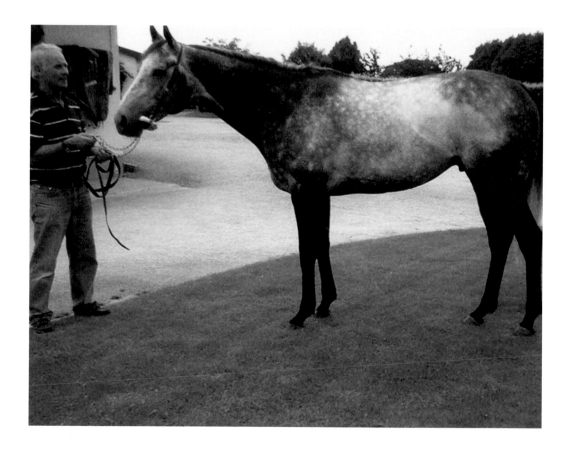

Above: Dermot Weld and his 1993 Melbourne Cup hero Vintage Crop *on their return from the epic race, the first Europeans to land Australia's great race.*

Right: Dublin-born Oscar winning film director Jim Sheridan, owner of one of Ireland's most popular Flat racehorses, Vinnie Roe.

Tom is not exactly slack when off duty, playing golf, swimming every night on his way home, and working in the garden.

Vinnie's owner was Oscar-winning film director Jim Sheridan, much of whose work has an Irish theme; films such as *In America, The Field, In the Name of the Father* and *Into the West* – about two boys and a horse – all deal with Ireland or the Irish. For Jim, a soft-spoken and helpful man, racing is a relaxing pastime. Jim is often in America, but when he is at home in Dublin with his wife, Fran, he is likely to have the big screen television tuned in to the racing channel 'attheraces' and to be in the company of his golden retriever and terrier.

Tom Gallagher describes him as 'a very nice man, down to earth, no airs or graces, he would chat away.'

Vinnie Roe, one of twins, was bred by Mrs Virginia Moeran by *Definite Article* out of

a mare by *Tap On Wood*, and could almost be said to be unprepossessing to look at, if that were not so derogatory. From the start *Vinnie* set the ball rolling in the determined fashion that became his trademark by winning his first race by a head; this was the only race in his career that was neither of Listed nor Group calibre. He ran three times as a two-year-old, finishing third and first after his debut, prompting Dermot Weld to tell the press, 'he is a good-actioned horse and could be a serious Group horse; he's tough, very much in the mould of his sire.'

He added that he looked forward to seeing him over ten furlongs as a three-year-old and hoped he 'might stay a mile and a half.'

As it happened, in his first race at that age he came up against one that was to become one of the greats, *Galileo* – and by virtue of having won a Listed race, *Vinnie* had to give him 3lbs. He finished third, and then fourth to him at the same venue, Leopardstown, in the Derby Trial, beaten in both by just over four lengths.

Rather than take on *Galileo* in the Epsom Derby it was off to the Italian Derby, where Tony Quinn deputised for Pat Smullen; the pair finished a not disgraced fourth of nineteen, considered good enough to take their chance in the Irish Derby, but it was *Galileo's* year, 2001, and *Vinnie Roe's* seventh of twelve reflected his 66-1 starting price.

He hadn't quite found his metier, but he was about to do so, and as *Vinnie Roe* stormed to victory in his next five consecutive races over a longer distance, Jim Sheridan's colours of distinctive dark blue with yellow stars became familiar to the racing public.

He stepped up in trip from 1½ miles to 1¾, confounding any stamina doubts that connections may originally have harboured, and the wins flowed: three weeks after the Irish Derby it was a Listed race at Leopardstown where he beat *Sadlers Wings* by four lengths; then a Listed race at the Curragh saw him pull out all the stops to beat *Pugin* by a head, a colt who had finished ahead of him in fourth place in the Irish Derby.

Now for the Irish St Leger. Traditionally, Classic races are for three-year-olds only, but in 1984 the Irish version of the St Leger, the autumn curtain-down, was opened up to all ages. *Vinnie Roe* had proved himself not quite good enough for a Derby, but the longer distance of the St Leger could suit, even though a three-year-old had not beaten the older horses since 1989. Crucially, it could also show whether or not he might be capable of contending the Melbourne Cup in Australia the following year. Dermot felt he had the temperament and constitution for such a test.

Opposite left: On his home ground and with his trademark effort, Vinnie Roe *wins at The Curragh.*
Below: Head man Tom Gallagher shares a joke with 'the equine love of his life' Vinnie Roe.

September 15, 2001, was *Vinnie Roe's* first launch on the Jefferson Smurfit Memorial (later Irish Field) Irish St Leger (Group 1), on good to firm ground, worth £105,604.84 to the winner. The English St Leger winner of 2000, *Millenary*, was favourite, and the ever popular *Persian Punch* was also running. (The consistent Irish-bred stayer won twenty races and placed nineteen times, but sadly he collapsed and died at the start of the 2004 season.)

Vinnie Roe was only a three-year-old, but he bucked the trend by beating his seniors, taking up the lead inside the final furlong and staying on well. *Millenary* had no answer to him in second place, and long time leader *Persian Punch* finished fourth behind *Marienbard*.

Dermot Weld told the press that he had deliberated intently on whether to keep *Vinnie Roe* in his own age group by sending him to Doncaster (for the English St Leger), or to take on the older horses at the Curragh. He had emphasised earlier in the week that it had been a desperately close call, and that no single factor had been responsible for the decision. However, after the race, he revealed the master-plan.

He said, 'I have had the Melbourne Cup in mind for him for some time, and for that reason I wanted to try him against the top-quality older horses. If he was to justify the journey, he had to beat a horse like *Persian Punch* who has already been to Melbourne. This gives us a good yardstick, because *Persian Punch* has run a fine race, and we have also beaten last year's St Leger winner.'

Vinnie Roe had established himself on the big Irish stage and so had his jockey, Pat Smullen, whose first Classic victory this was. The pair franked their positions by travelling to Longchamp six weeks later to win the French equivalent in convincing fashion.

So *Vinnie Roe* went into winter quarters having won his last four races as a three-year-old. The 2002 season started off in the same vein, when, under the welter burden of 10st 1lb and on soft ground, he won so well in Leopardstown that his next stop was a tilt at the Ascot Gold Cup. He looked like justifying favouritism, but was collared by *Royal Rebel* in a rousing finish under the superb Irish jockey Johnny Murtagh.

Afterwards, it was felt the 2½ miles was too far, and his 'guts, courage and stamina carried him through'.

He was given a break before his second tilt at the Irish St Leger; a first Melbourne Cup was also on the agenda. He achieved the first target in confident style, beating his old rival, *Pugin*.

Dermot was ecstatic: 'He is as tough and genuine as any horse I've trained and he doesn't know what it means to quit. This year he has matured in every way.'

So, could he conquer Australia? Owner Jim Sheridan was consulted. To send a horse all the way to Australia is expensive, not just the travelling or the race entry fee, but also the quarantine – to say nothing of the owner naturally wishing to travel himself. But it was too exciting a proposition to pass over. Jim agreed.

Dermot Weld also took *Media Puzzle* for Dr Michael Smurfit, but he had to qualify for the race first, which he did by winning a pre-Cup race in Australia. Even so, he carried a full stone less for the big one than *Vinnie Roe* who was top weight – and favourite.

There were twenty-three runners and, so long a preserve of the home team until Dermot Weld came along with Michael Smurfit's *Vintage Crop* in 1993, there were a number from overseas taking part this year, 2002. Saeed Bin Suroor had three runners, the best of which, *Bee Keeper*, finished third, plus Michael Stoute ran *Daliapour* ridden by Ireland's Mick Kinane, and Alan Jarvis also had a runner.

For Irish owners Jim Sheridan and Michael Smurfit, one a master of the arts, the other at the pinnacle of business, quiet, amenable men both, the moment of truth had come.

The Flemington, Melbourne, track glistened in the sunshine. The colourful flowers bloomed, the band played, and the 100,000-strong crowd paraded their high-fashion outfits and placed their bets. Melbourne on Cup day makes St Patrick's Day in Ireland look quiet.

Media Puzzle, a striking chestnut built more in the frame of a steeplechaser than a Flat horse, took a handy position early with *Vinnie* in about tenth, Pat Smullen mindful of the weight he had to carry. But with three furlongs to run, Pat moved *Vinnie* smoothly through to lead. His stable companion, ridden by Australian jockey Damien Oliver, tracked his move and took over two furlongs out, and, carrying a stone less for the two-mile marathon, went on to score. *Vinnie* ran his courageous heart out and was only relegated from second to fourth in the dying strides.

It was a great performance from both of Dermot Weld's horses who had famously said after his 1993 win that he would only return 'when he had one good enough.' He had just shown he probably had two.

For *Vinnie Roe* a deserved long holiday beckoned, and then a slightly more ambitious autumn plan: to try and win the Irish St Leger for a record-breaking third time and then, instead of going for the Melbourne Cup again, a first attempt at the Prix de l'Arc de Triomphe.

By now *Vinnie Roe* was five years old, an age when many colts have already gone off to stud, but *Vinnie* retained his zest for racing, winning his prep race by a gutsy head, before heading off for the Irish Field Irish St Leger once more. His many fans were not to be disappointed and there were hats in the air as he passed the post a length ahead of *Gamut*.

Not only connections, but also race-goers were delighted.

Dermot said, 'He is a true professional and a joy to train. I really believe there is more

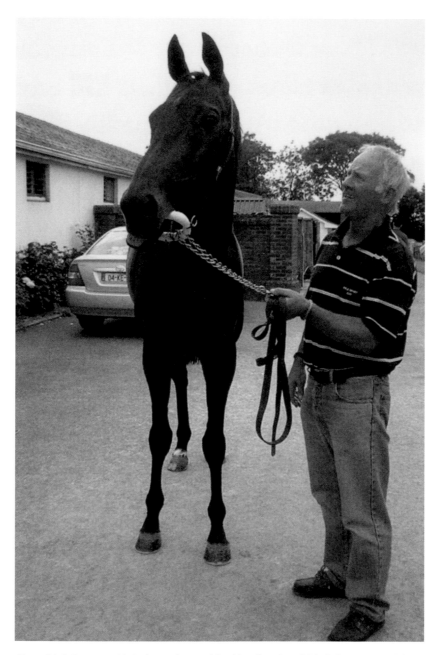

Above: Little in stature, big in heart, the record-breaking four-times Irish St Leger winner Vinnie Roe.

Above: Yes, four times: Pat Smullen salutes the crowd on one of his favourite horses, Vinnie Roe.

Above: The latest winning Weld: Eighteen-year-old Charles Weld, grandson of Dermot's uncle, John, rode his first winner in July 2008 on Battle In Hand. *The horse is owned by his mother, Michelle, seen here (left) with his father, also John (right).*

to come from this horse.'

Pat Smullen retains a soft spot for the horse that put him on the map. After the achievement of winning the race for a record third time, he said, 'I never had an anxious moment. He deserved to make history and riding a horse like him who wants to win so much makes it hard to lose; I owe this horse a lot, he has such guts and heart.'

After consulting the joint owners, it was off for Europe's most prestigious race, the Prix de l'Arc de Triomphe. 'Arc' day at Longchamp produces an incredible atmosphere, full of French chic, the huge crowds swelled by several thousand from Ireland and the UK. Betting is a Tote Monopoly so that all profits are ploughed back into racing, and nowhere does the advantage of this show itself better than at the beautifully-tended Longchamp. The wide course is manicured to perfection and in the smart stands are restaurants of a high standard. Many corporate and racing club packages are put together for the 'Arc' and it doesn't let them down. By coach, train, car, aeroplane or helicopter, it is a must in many racing fans' annual diary.

Racing is of the highest calibre, the supporting card giving justice to the 'Arc' as the race is universally known. It brings together Europe's very best horses, often including the current year's Derby winner taking on its older counterparts.

2003 was no exception. *Dalakhani* had suffered his only defeat, to *Alamshar* in the Irish Derby, and the year older *High Chaparral* had carried all before him when winning the Derby, Irish Derby, and Breeders' Cup Turf in his Classic year. He started favourite now, fresh from winning the Irish Champion Stakes; *Dalakhani* and the French-trained *Doyen* came next in the betting.

Dalakhani stamped his superiority by winning for the eighth time in nine starts, and *Vinnie Roe* was in no way disgraced, beaten less than nine lengths in fifth place.

He was to return to Longchamp three weeks later for an attempt to win the French St Leger for the second time. Not surprisingly he started favourite, but it was not to be and he finished fourth to *Westerner*.

With two prep runs, second in both, prior to his attempt on a fourth Irish Field Irish St Leger, there was a big following for *Vinnie Roe* on 18 September 2004 – and an even bigger cheer when he brought the improbable off, beating the useful *Brian Boru* by 2½ lengths. He had lifted the St Leger for an incredible fourth time and the cheers reached a crescendo as the crowds roared him home.

It was decided to return to Melbourne.

What a race was in store. In the intervening year since *Vinnie's* last visit, Australia's greatest race had been won by a then comparatively unknown mare called *Makybe Diva*.

But what a mare, as history was to prove. *Vinnie's* run behind her in 2004, beaten by just two lengths, grants him his place in posterity for that alone.

The dark blue and yellow stars adorning Pat Smullen were to have one more season on board the veteran. He comfortably won his first race of the 2005 season and then had a crack at the Ascot Gold Cup, run that year at York, where he was beaten into third by his old rival, *Westerner*. Another third saw him as ready as he could be for an incredible fifth attempt at the Irish St Leger. And when he forged into the lead two furlongs from home the packed grandstands roared, and roared and willed their hero to last home. He increased his lead and didn't slow up; but when the stout-hearted *Collier Hill* and *The Whistling Teal* challenged him, he could not find the extra, and he went under by a half a length and half a length; half a length behind him was the future top stayer, *Yeats*.

So Down Under once more for *Vinne Roe's* swansong – and victory to the mare again. *Vinnie Roe*, once more on top weight, this time jointly with *Makybe Diva*, was drawn on the outside; it was a swelteringly hot day and he might just as well have stayed in his stable.

Starting at 15-1 in a field of twenty-four, he tried as hard as ever, but could finish only eighth, about five lengths behind the great mare. It was probably as game a race as he ever ran because he was affected by the heat and finished distressed. Even so, he was best of the European runners.

Dermot said, 'He was dehydrated and we got fluids into him immediately. He ran his eyeballs out. I have never trained a more courageous horse.'

By his return to Ireland he once more looked a picture.

For *Makybe Diva*, conceived in Ireland and born in England, it was a record-breaking third Melbourne Cup.

So there was to be no fairy tale ending for *Vinnie Roe*. After a well-deserved break from his racing exertions, he began his new career at stud joining the roster of the National Hunt (NH) branch of Coolmore at Grange Stud.

For Tom Gallagher, going to visit *Vinnie* there one day, it set his heart thumping.

'He looked magnificent, I think he recognised me; he had been my pal from a yearling until the day he left. We still call his paddock at Dermot's the *Vinnie Roe*; he used to love being out there in the sun; he went out every day, he was entitled to it.'

Jim Sheridan said, 'The horse was named after Fran's brother, whose name is Vinnie Roe. He suffers from Down's Syndrome. He was born with a caul, which is associated with luck!'

Today there is another Charles Weld riding in the amateur ranks, the eighteen-year-old grandson of John and first cousin once removed to Dermot. In July 2008 Charles rode *Battle In Hand*, owned by his mother, Michelle, and trained by Dermot to win a twenty-runner bumper by a short head at – where else? – Galway.

THE DADDY OF THEM ALL – SADLER'S WELLS

WHEN BRAVE AND DARING ACE BATTLE OF BRITAIN and Far East fighter pilot Wing Commander Tim Vigors came home from World War II his family had inherited a middle-sized mixed farm near Fethard in Co. Tipperary; there they set up a small training establishment, typical of many in southern Ireland. The name of the farm was Coolmore.

The Vigors originated from Leighlinbridge in Co. Carlow (not far from where Willie Mullins trains today) where they had owned estates for centuries; Tim's brother, Terence, was Senior Steward of the Turf Club and the owner of Burgage Stud, Co. Carlow.

Rather than become part of the Fethard farm at that time, Tim joined Goffs Bloodstock Auctioneers and in 1948 he founded his own firm that in time was to become BBA (British Bloodstock Agency), as well known as any bloodstock agency in the world. Probably his most acclaimed sales brokerage was that of 1952 Derby winner *Tulyar* ('What did I tell-ya!' jockey Charlie Smirke famously called riding in on the Aga Khan's brown colt) from the Irish National Stud to a Kentucky syndicate. The sale was received with mixed feelings by the racing public and sporting press.

Firstly the sum of money was considered huge, $672,000, an American record for a stallion; and secondly, many in Ireland wanted his blood to remain on their soil. Bred in Kildare by the Aga Khan, *Tulyar* had been bought by the Irish Government for $700,000 at the end of his racing career in England which included winning the Epsom Derby. His services had been used for three years before Tim Vigors negotiated his sale in 1956; among those disappointed at the loss to Ireland were vet Dr Max Cosgrove and breeder and Jockey Club steward Frank Tuthill.

A large crowd gathered to bid *Tulyar* farewell; he was accompanied on the flight by Irish Stud groom of forty-four years Matthew Lynch, who had never been out of Ireland before.

Tim Vigors sold his shares in BBA in 1962, but having done so, he nevertheless remained a respected freelance agent and also a racing journalist and a vendor of Piper aeroplanes. He also loved to hunt; six years later he moved to the family farm and, fascinated as ever by thoroughbreds, set about turning it into a stud business.

By 1968 he began transforming it into a model stud farm, laying the foundations for the world-class and widely-acclaimed stud that it is today. About twenty-five years before that, on leave from his Spitfire squadron with the RAF, Tim accompanied his father racing in Mallow. Later, they went to see a friend's horses in training 'with a new young lad who is having a bit of success with very few horses.' Father and son were introduced to the 'small, neat figure' and shown the horses. Writing decades later in his memoir *Life's Too Short To Cry*, Tim recalls, 'They were all good sorts and looked in the best of health.' On the train journey back Tim's father, Major Vigors, asked two other trainers if they had heard of the new young trainer they had just met, one Vincent O'Brien.

'I did so,' replied one of the trainers, 'he's had a couple of winners lately and they say he's a bright young thing.'

So began Tim's friendship with possibly the greatest trainer of all time, and when he was trying to build up Coolmore it was to Vincent that he turned to help him achieve it. The pair became partners along with Robert Sangster, the Vernon's pools magnate and huge racing supporter and owner. Tim always said that one day it would be the best stud in Europe. Sadly he did not stay there long enough to realise his dream and in 1973 he bowed out of the Coolmore story. For personal reasons he sold his shares to Vincent O'Brien and Vincent's son-in-law, John Magnier (who in turn was later to become sole owner). The Vigors' name lives on in the racing and breeding world through Tim's great nephew, (Terence's grandson) Charlie Vigors, who rode about seventy winners when an assistant trainer for Nicky Henderson and runs a sales prep, breaking and mare boarding stud near Marlborough, Wiltshire. His wife, Tracy, grew up at Monksgrange Stud, Co. Wexford, where her father, Jack Wickham, was manager for Jeremy Hill.

✦ ✦ ✦

Opposite left: Vincent O'Brien, Robert Sangster, Lester Piggott 1979

COOLMORE STUD

The three men who were now, in the 1970s, jointly involved in Coolmore, Messrs O'Brien, Magnier and Sangster, brought different strengths into the business. They wanted to stand the best possible stallions, but those were in America, and if they had already proved themselves on the racecourse it would cost megabucks to buy them and bring them to Ireland. The defining moment was the conclusion that it would be cheaper – twenty times cheaper – to buy potential stallions as yearlings, race them and the most successful would stand at Coolmore. There would be some wastage, inevitably, but between them the men had wealth, a deep knowledge of bloodlines and, in Vincent, not only a wise man with an outstanding eye for a horse, but also a trainer to bring out the best in any animal. It meant they spread their investment, and reduced the gamble.

Robert Sangster's love affair with racing began when he was in his early thirties and he bought a racehorse for his first wife. It won, and the thrill and euphoria that followed had him hooked on racing for the rest of his life. He firstly bought Swettenham Stud in Cheshire, and then the historic Manton stables in Wiltshire. After Robert Sangster's death in 2004, aged sixty-seven, Vincent O'Brien told the BBC, 'Robert was a true visionary whose large-scale investment in the best American-bred yearlings in the seventies was one of the principal factors in establishing Ireland and Coolmore as major forces in the bloodstock world.'

Below: Northern Dancer, *sire of* Sadler's Wells *and a remarkable racehorse himself, was tiny, as shown here in the 1980s with Richard, Duc de Stacpoole, of Roundstone, Connemara.*
Opposite top: The greatest daddy, Sadler's Wells.

The racing world turned out in force to pay tribute to Dr Vincent O'Brien when he died in Derby Week, June 2009. He was ninety-two years old and was widely attributed with having turned around the world of racing in Ireland; many spoke of him as 'being ahead of his time.' It was his attention to detail, forward planning, meticulous care and above all his eye for a horse that stood him apart.

John Magnier, an astute, private man of many parts, built the farm into the multinational, multi-billion-euro operation that operates worldwide today. The original farm is now known as Coolmore Ireland, and has two branches overseas, Ashford Stud known as Coolmore America operating from near Versailles, Kentucky; and Coolmore Australia, based near Jerry's Plains, in the Hunter Valley of New South Wales. With operations in both the Northern and Southern Hemispheres, Coolmore has numerous world-class 'shuttle stallions' that cover mares in either Ireland or Kentucky in the northern breeding season and are transported to Australia for the southern breeding season.

Long gone, it seems, are the days when a stallion's full book for a season was forty mares. Then it increased to eighty. With the shuttle service a top stallion today will be covering up to 350 mares, enjoying two seasons in one calendar year. An improvement in veterinary science is one reason for this as, with precise timing of the mare, usually one cover is enough.

One of their first NH stallions to put Coolmore well and truly on the map was *Deep*

Above: Sadler's Wells *retired in 2008, but still enjoys youthful gallops in the paddock.*

Run, (sire of *Dawn Run* and numerous other winners); he was champion sire for fourteen consecutive years. There is a story that in the 1980s so many mares were being returned as 'in foal to *Deep Run*' that a monitor/spy/call-him-what-you-will was dispatched from Weatherby's in England to glean the truth of the huge numbers; one story is that he was put into a cold and bare hut, another that he stayed in the best nearby hotel; whatever, he didn't stay long – but probably long enough to learn that *Deep Run* was indeed a very, very busy sire...

There is much more than luck to the success of Coolmore. Money and astute business skills have turned the rural Tipperary farm into a world phenomenon. It has not been achieved by fluke but by meticulous attention to detail, reminiscent of Vincent O'Brien's own training philosophy.

One stallion did more than any other to stamp Coolmore's success: *Sadler's Wells*. He could be called the 'daddy of them all'.

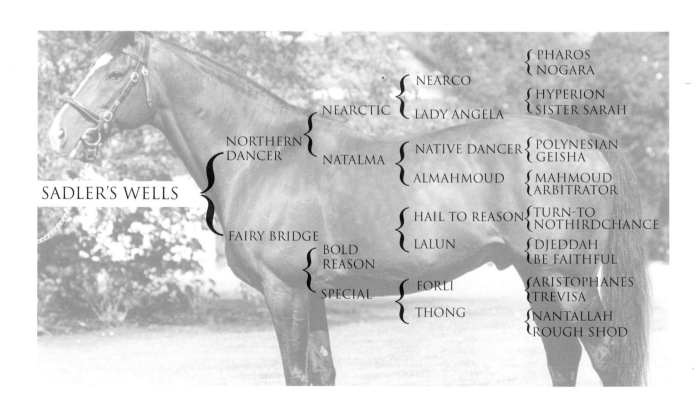

Above: Sadler's Wells *wins the 1984 Irish 2,000 Guineas at the Curragh for trainer Vincent O'Brien.*

NORTHERN DANCER

Sadler's Wells was by *Northern Dancer*, the Canadian horse who was far and away the best thoroughbred to come out of that country. In 1952, Edward P. Taylor, a Canadian business magnate and owner of Windfields Farm, Ontario, attended the Newmarket December sales where he purchased *Lady Angela*, a mare in foal to leading English-based sire *Nearco*. The following spring, Taylor sent *Lady Angela* to *Nearco* once again, and then shipped her to his farm in Canada later in 1953; in 1954, *Lady Angela* foaled a colt in Canada named *Nearctic* who was voted the 1958 Sovereign Award for Horse of the Year. From *Nearctic* and the mare *Natalma* (by *Native Dancer*), came *Northern Dancer*, a late foal, born on 27 May 1961.

Northern Dancer was so small, barely 14.3hh, that he didn't realise his $25,000 dollar reserve as a yearling, and so he joined his owner's Windfield Farm racing stables. He soon proved that lack of size was no barrier to success. At two, his seven victories in nine starts earned him the Canadian Juvenile Championship. In his two years of racing, *Northern Dancer* won fourteen of his eighteen races and never finished worse than third; he narrowly missed out on winning America's Triple Crown, taking the first two legs of Kentucky Derby and Preakness Stakes, but finished third in the Belmont Stakes. He was trained throughout his career by Horatio Lure and mostly ridden by Bill Hartack after Willie Shoemaker had opted not to ride him in the Kentucky Derby.

As a stallion, by which time it is said he had grown to 15.1¾, *Northern Dancer* proved every bit as successful as on the racecourse. He sired the great *Nijinsky* and other Derby winners such as *Secreto* and *The Minstrel*, as well as Irish Derby winners *El Gran Senor* and *Shareef Dancer*. His influence as a stallion is still strongly felt in Classic races throughout the world. His sons who became great sires included *Nureyev, Lyphard, Danzig, Storm Bird* and, of course, *Sadler's Wells*.

Northern Dancer is also the paternal grandsire of several prominent stallions, including *Storm Cat, El Prado* and *Danehill*, among others. He is the great grandsire (on both the sire and dam side) of *Big Brown*, the winner of the 2008 Kentucky Derby and Preakness Stakes. He is the great-great-grandsire (on both the sire and dam side) of *Mine That Bird*, the shock winner of the 2009 Kentucky Derby, and *Rachel Alexandra*, the winner of the 2009 Kentucky Oaks and Preakness Stakes. *Northern Dancer* won many awards both during and after his life (including some years later a Canadian postage stamp). If he was the twentieth

Below: John Magnier, Vincent O'Brien's son-in-law and a major player in the Coolmore enterprise.

century's sire of sires it is likely that his son, *Sadler's Wells* will bear that accolade for the twenty-first.

SADLER'S WELLS

Sadler's Wells was officially bred by Robert Sangster's Swettenham Stud, but he was born in America, to a mare called *Fairy Bridge*, the joint top rated two-year-old filly in Ireland in 1977 when she won both her races, the only two starts of her career. By *Bold Reason*, the American-bred mare was bought relatively cheaply by the partners in Coolmore; she was also the dam of *Fairy King*, another top sire.

Sadler's Wells won a Derby trial, but not a Derby. His wins came at trips of seven to ten furlongs. In his Classic year, as a three-year-old, he won the Irish 2,000 Guineas; the Eclipse Stakes at Sandown; the Irish Champion Stakes; and the Derrinstown Stud Derby Trial. He was also second in the 'King George' (to *Teenoso*); the Prix du Jockey Club (to *Darshaan*); and the Gladness Stakes at the Curragh (to *El Gran Senor*). Faint praise could best describe some reports of the time: for his Irish 2000 Guineas win in 1984, jockey Pat Eddery preferred Robert Sangster's other runner. *Sadler's Wells* beat *Procida* and *Secreto* a neck and half a length, prompting this from the *Irish Field* correspondent: 'As the first six were divided by less than three lengths there is a distinct possibility that this was a sub-standard classic.' The writer did go on to say that he did not subscribe to that view.

Sadler's Wells had a very good record, but he truly came into his own as a stallion. His progeny reads like an *aide memoire* to all that was, and is, the best in thoroughbred racing for two decades, both on the Flat and in NH.

To look at, *Sadler's Wells* is a model racehorse, the epitome of all that is good about the thoroughbred. A rich bay, dappled when the sun shines, with black legs and two white hind socks and white blaze, he stands 15.3hh and has show-horse conformation. He has so dominantly imparted his genes to the mares that visit him that frequently one can look at a horse and know instantly that it is by *Sadler's Wells*. More importantly, they keep winning, winning – and adding to the gene pool, a huge number becoming successful sires themselves, under both codes.

Who can forget *Montjeu* and his fabulous 'Arc' win? Or Derby winner *Galileo* – both established successful stallions. *Montjeu* already has two Derby winners to his credit, *Authorised* and *Motivator*, and in 2009 *Fame and Glory* by *Montjeu* won the Irish Derby. *Galileo*, a chip off the old block, has sired Derby winner *New Approach* and was the leading sire on prize-money won in the UK and Ireland for 2008.

Those are only a start. Forgive the list, but how else to include even some of *Sadler's Wells'* great sons? Many of them have become leading sires themselves, both Flat and NH, and so continued the successful bloodline; there are many on the distaff side, too. Among a plethora of Classic winners *Sadler's Wells* has produced Irish 2,000 Guineas winners *Barathea* and *Saffron Walden*; Irish Derby: *Old Vic* (now a leading NH sire); *Dream Well* and *Salsabil*; 2,000 Guineas: *King of Kings* and *Refuse To Bend*; St Leger: *Milan*, (NH sire), and *Brian Boru*; and *Alexandrova* (Oaks and Irish Oaks).

Then there is *Yeats*, an out and out stayer, who won a record-breaking fourth Ascot Gold Cup in 2009; the massive crowds gave him a standing ovation as Johnny Murtagh paraded him past the stands – and behind the scenes, the lads gave him a guard of honour as he returned to the stable yard. *Kayf Tara* won two Ascot Gold Cups; and then there are Prix de l'Arc de Triomphe winners, *Montjeu* and *Carnegie*. He has also sired many winners

Below: 'Classic Moments at the Curragh', September 2008, Vincent and Jacqueline O'Brien with son Charles, right, and grandchildren Andrew and Elizabeth.

in America.

And there is one particular gelding to be mentioned, the triple Champion Hurdler *Istabraq*. Not the success he should have been on the Flat, *Istabraq's* story when he turned to hurdling has many emotional strands that have rightly made his own book.

He was ridden in all twenty-nine of his hurdle races by Charlie Swan, and the partnership won twenty-three of them; in two of his three seconds he went under by a head (in the other, at 7-1 on, he was beaten five lengths by *Limestone Lad*); he had two falls; and on the final outing of his illustrious career he was pulled up. But for the loss of Cheltenham 2001 due to foot and mouth there is every reason to believe he would have won four Champion Hurdles.

These horses will evoke different memories for diverse people, of great races, easy wins, hard fought battles; they have one thing in common – they were all by *Sadler's Wells*.

It was only in 2008, at the age of twenty-seven, that *Sadler's Wells* was finally retired from stud duties. His illustrious father was *Northern Dancer*; his successor may well be *Galileo*. The value of their blood to the racing industry is priceless.

Sadler's Wells' retirement brought numerous tributes, including this from Leo Powell, managing editor of the *Irish Field*: 'When you have used every superlative in the dictionary, what is the next option? Keep it simple perhaps. Let's just say that he was great. Now it is time to remind oneself not to write in the past tense. *Sadler's Wells* may be retired, embarking on a well-earned rest in Coolmore, his home for some twenty-four years. However, he is very much part of the landscape that is world racing and breeding. Few horses have ever made the impact on the breed that he has. Some have tried and even come close. None have been better though. A multiple champion, his influence on the world of thoroughbred breeding and racing is incalculable … The good news is that the story is still unfolding, and for the next couple of decades we can expect to talk about him and his sons, grandsons and great-grandsons and their successes. His record as a broodmare sire is also making for impressive reading, and his emergence in recent times as a multiple champion in that sphere is also set to grow in stature and frequency.

'… Not only has *Sadler's Wells* been a kingpin down in Tipperary. But his contribution to Ireland's development as a major breeding centre of excellence should not be underestimated. His success fuelled the growth of Coolmore, while bringing the *crème de la crème* of the world's broodmares to this country to be covered and to reside.'

TWO GREAT RIDING BROTHERS –

TIM AND MARTIN MOLONY

BROTHERS TIM AND MARTIN MOLONY were iconic riders whose names became bywords among racing aficionados in the 1940s and 1950s. Tim was champion NH jockey in England five times between 1948 and 1955, and Martin, whose career was cut short, was equally effective on the Flat as over jumps, winning Classics and a Gold Cup. He was champion jockey in Ireland from 1946 to 1951.

'BUFFALO BILL'

The Molony family has been a part of Meanus, Co. Limerick life for seven generations, with at least the last four steeped in the country traditions of farming, hunting, racing and breeding.

There are references to the family dating back to 1682 in the Manister parish. Rathmore

Left: Brothers Tim (left) and Martin Molony from County Limerick were crack riders of their day, seen here at Belmont Park, USA, in 1950.

House was built in the 1840s by Timothy Molony, great-grandfather of the current incumbent, Peter Molony. Timothy was married to Mary and their son, William – Tim and Martin's father – was something of a character; he spent years travelling in the Wild West, earning the name 'Buffalo Bill'. Once home he loved nothing more than to be hunting and racing across the Limerick countryside; he owned and trained *Hill of Camas*, named after a Molony out-farm, to win the 1915 Galway Plate, ridden by neighbour and life-long friend George Harty.

William was already getting on in years, comparatively, when he joined up with the Munster Fusiliers, so men were not too keen to serve under him at first, especially when they heard of his nickname, 'Buffalo Bill'. But soon news spread that the captain never seemed to get his men into trouble; the secret was his 'eye' for a country, from his years of hunting. Where other officers got disorientated, without fail, Captain Molony brought his men safely back to their trenches. He had the highest survival rate, and he also won the Military Cross for bravery when, under fire, he used horses to pull out vehicle-propelled guns that were stuck in the mud.

When William returned to Rathmore he was unusual in that he was a Catholic Irish farmer who was also a staunch Unionist and a magistrate.

He remained a formidable character and his methods of breaking in horses during the 1920s were reminiscent of his earlier Wild West cowboy lifestyle, in which finesse or patience might not have played too great a part. With one of them, *Timber Wolf*, he set about winning a second Galway Plate in 1936 and very nearly pulled it off. The grey was leading when he fell at the last fence; after subsequent chase wins he was bought by J.V. Rank and went on to win the 1938 Welsh Grand National.

William married Kate (Kitty) O'Connell, an attractive woman who was a skilled rider and enjoyed hunting, always riding side-saddle. The couple had eight children, though only six survived childhood: Tim, Mary who lives in Cornwall, Peg (married to well-known Limerick horseman Michael Leonard), Martin (who was six years younger than Tim), Kittens, twins who died at birth and Jack, who died aged seven from meningitis.

MARTIN

Tim and Martin loved hunting, although Martin recalls falling off six different ponies in

Above: Greenogue *(Martin Molony up), just leads* Whispering Steel *(Tim Molony) with* Pen-y-Don *(R. Turnell) behind.* Greenogue, *owned by J. V. Rank, wins the Fairmile Chase at Sandown Park, 1951.*

one day. But the experience made a horseman of him and he was hard to dislodge from the saddle once he took up racing (a bit like Paul Carberry today). Tim, equally, was known as 'the rubber man' because he always seemed to be able to walk away from falls, and was fearless riding into a last fence. He only once broke a bone – his leg – in his last racing fall in 1958.

In the 1940s, the brothers bought a horse called *Knight's Crest* that ran in their mother's name and was trained by their friend Captain Cyril (C.B.) Harty. *Knight's Crest* won the 1944 Irish Grand National with Martin Molony in the saddle, beating the great *Prince Regent*. Martin, who had been apprenticed to Captain Harty on the Flat, was only eighteen years old.

Tim and Martin, as different in nature as chalk and cheese, were as close as twins and were best friends throughout their lives. Martin's son, Peter (who is Tim's godson), says, 'Tim was the outgoing one who loved wine and women, Martin never smoked or drank and was much quieter.

'Tim used to look after Martin on the English racecourses. The only Irish racing was on a Saturday so Martin travelled over a lot. One time Tim was injured and so not there to warn him when a particular trainer came into the weighing room looking for a rider for his horse. The other jockeys, knowing the horse's reputation, scattered. Martin rode the horse and won. Afterwards he discovered it had fallen in its five previous runs.'

Their different characters were reflected in their riding styles: Martin was a more sympathetic rider and more of a stylist, probably helped by the flat racing in which he was very neat.

Tim and Martin frequently rode in the same race and on a number of occasions found themselves disputing the lead together at the last fence.

As the eldest son, Tim inherited Rathmore, but England had become his home – he'd made his career there, he'd married there and settled down – so he sold Rathmore to Martin.

Martin had already retired from racing when he married Julia Hilton-Green, whose father, Chetty, was a renowned English huntsman and Master, famous for his years with the Cottesmore and also the North Cotswold and other packs. He showed excellent sport, his hounds adored him and so did the people around him. He simply loved hunting, had a huge zest for life, and was a charming and witty raconteur. Not surprisingly, he married into another hunting family, Lady Helena Fitzwilliam, known as 'Boodley'. However, the marriage ended in divorce and Lady Helena later married Lord Daresbury, formerly Master

Below: Mr and Mrs R. K. Mellon, leading US owners, with Martin Molony c. 1947.

Above: Red Rum *and Tommy Stack. Bred in Ireland,* Red Rum *was spotted as a yearling and trained for a while by Tim Molony.*

of the Belvoir Hunt in Leicestershire and then of the Limerick; so it was that Julia found herself with her mother and step-father in Ireland – and in 1960 married Martin Molony.

Martin speaks of Julia, to whom he has been married for forty-nine years, simply as 'my wonderful wife.'

They had four children, Peter, Mary, Jan and Susannah, of whom Peter rode in one charity race and Mary was a keen point-to-point rider on *Any Crack*, trained by P.P. Hogan.

TIM

Tim Molony began riding as an amateur in 1936 and won about a hundred point-to-points including over banks and walls; he turned professional in 1940, just as racing was curtailed due to the War.

Tim's choice to stay in England eventually served him well, but initially it was not easy. A slow start in 1946 was made even slower by the interminable, snow-bound winter of 1947, when many parts of the British Isles experienced record low temperatures and snow cover from January to March. Added to that, his wife, Isobel (nee Bowe), whom he had married in 1945, was gravely ill. His 'little brother', champion in Ireland, seemed to win every time he travelled to England. The stable Tim was riding for was dispersed and his future looked glum.

At last he got the breaks that he needed, and during the 1950s he won the Gold Cup, four consecutive Champion Hurdles, and many big chases including three Seftons at Aintree and three Great Yorkshires at Doncaster; he was champion jockey in Britain five times, consecutively from 1948-52 and finally 1954-55.

Like his brother, Tim was a horseman as well as jockey, but he was probably the more pugnacious of the two. Of a heavier build than Martin, his career was always in jumping. Once his bandwagon began to roll he ended up riding about nine hundred winners for many different trainers by the time he retired in 1958. It was to be 1972 before Stan Mellor broke the 1,000 barrier, since when a handful of others have achieved it – and one, A.P. (Tony) McCoy notched up his staggering 3000th winner in February 2009.

It was Irish genius trainer Vincent O'Brien who trained two of Tim's most prestigious winners. The families had long known each other and Tim went to school with Vincent and his younger brother Dermot, with whom Tim shared a desk.

Hatton's Grace had already won the Champion Hurdle twice under Aubrey Brabazon when Tim came in for the ride in 1951 to make it three in a row. He had a tougher time two years later when lining up for the Cheltenham Gold Cup on the versatile *Knock Hard*. The horse had won the Irish Lincolnshire and throughout his long career successfully

Above: Martin Molony – combined sympathy and great strength in a finish, both on the Flat and over fences.

mixed Flat racing with hurdling and steeplechasing; but although he did win the 1953 Cheltenham Gold Cup, Tim was adamant that *Knock Hard* didn't like jumping fences. The horse had been badly frightened when virtually spread-eagling at his first chase fence, in the 'King George' at Kempton on Boxing Day no less! He finished third and in the Gold Cup he was well behind, not enjoying it; Tim persevered and, as with *Knock Hard's* other chases, once there were no more fences to be jumped, he sprinted up the run-in.

When he won this Gold Cup Tim also scored the middle of three Champion Hurdle victories on *Sir Ken*, trained by Willie Stephenson. He had come over from France as a four-year-old in 1951 and swiftly served notice of his class and potential with a runaway win in a hurdle at Aintree on Grand National Day. From then until the autumn of 1953 he remained unbeaten in sixteen races. By the time the 1954 Champion Hurdle came round he was no longer quite so dominant, but with his fluent hurdling and Tim's handling the pair were not to be denied: three in a row for *Sir Ken* and a remarkable four running for Tim.

Sadly, Isobel's illness proved fatal and a few years later, in 1951, Tim re-married, to an English girl, Stella Birch. In time, they produced sons Will, Marty and Danny, brothers for his daughter from his first marriage, Patricia. They made their home in England, finally at Wymondham, in the heart of the Leicestershire hunting country around Melton Mowbray, from where Tim trained and lived from 1960 until his death in 1991.

So Tim had a riding record that remains up there with the best of them throughout the history of steeplechasing.

MORE MARTIN

And Martin? The Cheltenham Gold Cup. Two Irish Classics. Third in the Epsom Derby; short-head second in the Irish Derby. Three Irish Nationals. Two Ulster Nationals and an Ulster Derby. That jumping and Flat Classics came alike illustrates the versatility of one of Ireland's riding legends, a fame that was honoured more than half a century after he hung up his racing boots when Martin, in his eighties, was presented with the Irish Thoroughbred Breeders Association Lifetime Achievement Award.

Always lightweight, Martin Molony signed on as an apprentice in Wiltshire, England, when his wage of two shillings and sixpence a week (12 ½ pence) plus keep left him with enough to visit the cinema in Marlborough.

'But I cried for the first week I was there, I was so lonely,' Martin recalls.

He rode his first gallop alongside Gordon Richards, later knighted, on the very day that World War II broke out. As a result of 'the Emergency', he and the other Irish apprentices travelled home.

Martin was soon riding winners, the first of which was *Chitor* in Phoenix Park. His most memorable moment was his marvellous win in the 1951 Cheltenham Gold Cup aboard Lord Bicester's course specialist *Silver Fame*. It was a great finish, in which three jumped the last in line abreast, *Silver Fame*, *Lockerbie* and *Greenogue*. *Lockerbie* blundered, but *Silver Fame* and *Greenogue* remained locked in combat the whole way up that famous hill. At the finish, though, Martin Molony and *Silver Fame*, who still holds the record number of eleven wins at Cheltenham, were not to be denied.

Martin's own favourite race is one he did not win but nevertheless is rightly proud of. He was riding Dorothy Paget's *Happy Home* in the 1948 Cheltenham Gold Cup. Coming to the last, Martin knew his only chance of beating Vincent O'Brien's *Cottage Rake*, with Aubrey Brabazon up, was to conjure a mighty leap from his mount. He gave it his all, the horse responded and must have gained a length in the air; immediately Martin gathered him up and the pair galloped for home. Even though *Cottage Rake* – who was to win the next two Gold Cups as well – had too much turn of foot and wore him down to win the race, the memory of that leap is still a fond one.

Martin also recalls the time he rode seven consecutive jumping winners: one at Sandown, followed by five in Navan, and then it was into the winner's enclosure again on his next ride in Leicester. Seven in a row – and precious few jumping jockeys will ever have achieved that. There was another time when, between January and Cheltenham, he won nineteen races out of twenty-three rides for Tom Dreaper.

His convincing win on *Signal Box* in the 1951 Irish 2,000 Guineas earned him a tilt at the Epsom Derby, where in a scrap for the minor places, they finished third. Hopes for winning the Irish Derby were high — and he blamed himself for a three-quarter-length defeat by the Epsom Derby winner *Frais du Bois II*.

Martin recalls, 'I came a bit too soon, I got impatient. I'd been told to ride a waiting race, but in the race Jimmy Eddery [father of Pat] called over "What are you doing back here?" and Charlie Smirke caught me on the post.'

In addition to *Knight's Crest* in 1944 Martin also won the 1946 Irish National on Mrs L. Lillingstone's *Golden View*, and in 1950 he won it again on Mrs P. Kiely's *Dominick's Bar* trained by Tim Hyde.

Of today's jockeys, Martin calls Tony McCoy 'a wonderful rider'. Many of yesterday's racing fans recall Martin as being ahead of his time, totally dedicated, teetotal, and combining flat-race polish in a NH finish; to them, he was the supreme stylist of the post-war years.

He was also well up for fun, and loved nothing more than to swim in the sea straight after Tramore races, then the only four-day festival in Ireland, or to go dancing.

Inevitably he took his share of falls, too, but medical checks were scarce then. One contemporary remembers him being 'drilled into the ground' in Tramore — yet there he was swimming away the soreness shortly after.

And he would ride again straight after a fall if at all possible, following the motto, 'it's very hard to get to the top, but very easy to slip off.'

He is remembered for his strength in a finish and could seem to be giving a horse a very hard race over the last three fences, yet that horse would return home with barely a whip mark on him — and would have won, too.

It was shortly after his victory in the Gold Cup that a crunching fall in Thurles brought a premature end to his illustrious career. His skull was broken (as well as a leg) and he had a year off. After that, he had the choice of being first jockey to Vincent O'Brien for NH or for Darkie Prendergast on the Flat.

He spent the year of his convalescence back home at Rathmore and he found he didn't miss the hectic racing schedule, especially the constant travelling to and fro between Ireland and England. There was only one way he could race and that was the hard-driven way. He chose to stay home, tend to the farm, buy and sell a few young thoroughbreds, and run one or two brood mares. Among the good horses he bred were *Skindles Hotel*, the champion Irish two-year-old of 1956; Royal Ascot winner *Brocade Slipper*; *Clara Bow*, who won three Flat races, and *Romping To Work* who won three German Champion Hurdles. Another was

Above: Martin's son, Peter, runs Rathmore Stud, Co. Limerick, seen here with a youngster out of a half sister to dual Champion Hurdler Hardy Eustace.

Above: Martin Molony, who was Champion Jockey from 1946 to 1951, chats with current Champion, Ruby Walsh and Barry Geraghty (left) in the jockeys' changing room before the Guinness Kerry National, Listowel, 2007.

Tumvella, who produced black-type-winning NH progeny.

This was also the period when he met and married Julie.

In later years, he and Tim were responsible for buying two yearlings that reached the top of their respective games, the Champion Hurdler *Bula*, and the immortal triple Grand National winner, *Red Rum*, who Tim also trained for a period from his Leicestershire base.

Today Martin and Julia live at Ottersfield about a mile and a half from Rathmore, which is now run by their son, Peter.

PETER MOLONY

After his racing career ended, Martin only took up riding again when Peter, aged about eleven, decided to start hunting on the pony, *Misty*, on which his three younger sisters were already keen riders. Martin was despatched to 'mind' Peter in the hunting field – but once hounds found, that was it, Martin was gone with them, the old adrenalin pumping as hard as ever.

'I was taken under the wing of two kindly ladies, Merry Atkinson and Susie Hogan, P.P. (Pat) Hogan's daughter,' Peter recalls.

Peter's own racing career numbers one charity race at the old Limerick racecourse, and it is the stud that he has concentrated on. After attending Gurteen Agricultural College and the Irish National Stud course in Kildare, he set off for the big studs of Kentucky, USA, and then on to Australia and New Zealand for about three years.

'I loved it, but when I returned I wanted to bring in new ideas.'

Inevitably that can be difficult for the older generation to latch on to and so Peter set up on his own, renting a farm nearby and setting out on his embryonic breeding career – with great success.

After he married Sarah Cleary, his parents moved to their present home and Peter and Sarah took over Rathmore. They have three young children, Sam, Tim and Kate.

Outside Peter has built on an additional forty stables and he has become a dual purpose breeder, roughly 50 per cent Flat and 50 per cent NH. Over the last ten years, he's had about twenty winners, split quite evenly between Flat and NH. He also 'pin-hooks' foals to sell on as yearlings, with considerable success.

'My biggest supporter from day one has been David Minton [the bloodstock agent]; he bought my first foal as a yearling and it won the Grade 2 Reynoldstown Chase at Ascot; he was called *The Toiseach*.' (Apparently, the name was misspelled at registration – he was intended to be called *The Taoiseach*).

David Minton also bought *Rising Cross*, a filly who finished second in the Oaks and won the Park Hill Stakes. In 2008 he bought eight or nine young horses from Peter and a year later two of them had already won bumpers, including *Quantitativeeasing* on the opening day of the Punchestown Festival, in the hands of J.P. Magnier.

On one occasion Peter was able to buy a daughter of Martin's *Tumvella* to continue the line, *Aon Dochas*, and she bred a number of winners. Another he bought is the 2001 Hong Kong Derby winner *Sobriety*; and also current top class sprinter *Tax Free*.

Peter, like his father, plainly loves the place and is steeped in the whole tradition of Rathmore. He is not only 'hands on' at home, but is also NH committee chairman for the Irish Thoroughbred Breeders Association.

Martin Molony sums up the whole family (and many Irishmen and women), when he says, 'I love the land – God's creation that feeds us all – and I love the horse. The horse is a wonderful animal, I love their every breath.'

Above: Nat Galway-Greer (on champion show hunter Mighty Fine*) was responsible for the sale of* Golden Miller *from Ireland to the UK.*

GOLDEN MILLER AND THE GERAGHTYS

THE STORY OF *GOLDEN MILLER'S* BIRTH REALLY BEGINS fourteen years before it, just before the outbreak of World War I in 1914.

The setting is a family farm at Pelletstown near Drumree in Co. Meath, in the heart of the Meath and Ward Union hunting countries. The range of stables is a few feet from the back door of the farmhouse and the owner, Lawrence Geraghty senior, keeps a National Hunt mare and a hunter along with his sheep and cattle. One day an acquaintance, a Jewish businessman, brought a mare in for grass livery. Then war broke out and the businessman vanished. No bills were paid and no contact was established, nothing.

In time, Lawrence Geraghty and his son, also Lawrence, began breeding from the mare, who was called *Miller's Pride*. She was a good breeder and produced a foal most years, some of whom went on to win some races after being sold as yearlings.

In 1927 she was due to foal to a stallion called *Goldcourt* and the Geraghtys, father and son, took out an oil lamp to the large foaling stable that was detached from the main block. Head man Jimmy McCann assisted the mare, but in her labours her hind leg knocked over

GOLDEN MILLER (1927)

GOLDCOURT
{
GOLDMINER
{
GALLINULE
{
ISONOMY
MOORHEN
SEEK AND FIND
{
GOLDSEEKER
BIDE-A-WEE
POWERSCOURT
{
ATHELING
{
STERLING
KING TOM MARE
WATERFALL
{
ARBITRATOR
MILLWHEEL

MILLER'S PRIDE
{
WAVELET'S PRIDE
{
FERNANDEZ
{
STERLING
ISOLA BELLA
WAVELET
{
PAUL JONES
WANDA
MILLER'S DAUGHTER
{
QUEEN'S BIRTHDAY
{
HAGIOSCOPE
MATILDA
ALLAN WATER
{
BARCALDINE
THIRLMERE

the lamp; so the bay colt foal with the attractive white star was born in the dark.

So the Geraghty family bred, *de facto*, the horse with the best Gold Cup record of all: five Gold Cups in six years with the intervening year lost to the weather. *Cottage Rake, Arkle* and *Best Mate* all won three. For these later three horses, the Gold Cup was the recognised blue riband of the sport, being a 'level playing field' competed for off the same weight. In *Golden Miller's* time, the Gold Cup was a prep race for the Grand National, a handicap, the prize money for which was more than ten times that of the Gold Cup.

It is right that the Geraghtys are recognised as *Golden Miller's* breeders. The following year, when *Golden Miller* was a yearling, Jimmy McCann walked him to the Goffs sales then held in Sewells Yard, Mount Street, Dublin. Jimmy's wages at the time were probably about 30/– (£1.50) per week, so the £100 raised at the sale was quite a good price.

The buyer was Paddy Quinn who turned the yearling out on his Tipperary farm with a number of others to grow and to mature for a couple of years.

Meanwhile, a couple of *Golden Miller's* half brothers were doing well in England; one of them, *May Court*, had won five races for a young trainer called Basil Briscoe and was fancied for the Grand National. Lawrence Geraghty received a call from Nat Galway Greer enquiring if he had any more coming along. The dam, *Miller's Pride*, had died in foal the following year, so not only was *Golden Miller* her last foal, but also there was none of his female bloodline left.

Lawrence directed Nat Greer to Paddy Quinn who duly bought the three-year-old on behalf of English trainer Basil Briscoe for £500 and the gawky youngster headed over the water to England.

Basil Briscoe, an old Etonian, trained from the family home, Longstowe in Cambridgeshire (he was also a joint-Master of the Cambridgeshire Harriers). About a year before *Golden Miller* came into his care Basil Briscoe was part owner of *Elton*, the 100/1 winner of the 1929 Lincolnshire Handicap. In 1935, when he had parted company with Dorothy Paget and her fabled chaser, he was also part-owner and trainer of *Commander III*, winner of that year's Cambridgeshire, netting him £10,000 in bets which gave him the means to get married. Horses were involved in both the best and the worst times of Basil Briscoe's life, and he was never the same after the *Golden Miller* affair. Going head to head with the redoubtable Dorothy Paget in a very public row over the horse seemed to take its toll on his health; when he died in 1951 he was only forty-eight years old.

But in 1930, when the unfurnished Irish youngster arrived, the best years of his life were ahead of him.

At first neither Basil Briscoe nor his stable staff was impressed with *Golden Miller*. By some accounts, his first race at Southwell was so unimpressive that he was sent hunting – and still found to be too slow! Worse, he took the fences by the roots.

But he matured and improved and before long Briscoe made a quick profit, selling him to one of his owners, Philip Carr, who shelled out £1,000 for him. He soon recouped this sum and more, for the growing 'ugly duckling' won two quick races, over hurdles at Leicester and Nottingham, and placed in others. In his first chase he was beaten a head by the favourite, and the following autumn he ran in four hurdles, winning two. Philip Carr's purchase was proving a success. Sadly, he became terminally ill and instructed that his horses be sold.

Enter Dorothy Paget. She asked Basil Briscoe if he had any good horses for sale.

'I have the best chaser in the world and the best hurdler in England,' he declared, and sold her *Golden Miller* and *Insurance* for £10,000 (or £12,000 according to some reports) for the pair.

It was no idle boast. *Insurance* won the next two Champion Hurdles, 1932-33, (a race Dorothy Paget was to win twice more, with *Solford* in 1940 and *Distel*, 1946); and *Golden Miller* was to win an unprecedented five Cheltenham Gold Cups and one Grand National.

WILL HE WIN THE "NATIONAL" AGAIN?

Miss Dorothy Paget's Golden Miller in Action

GOLDEN MILLER : By Goldcourt—Miller's Pride, by Wavelet's Pride. The photograph was taken at Leicester when "The Miller" had little more than gentle exercise in disposing of five other moderate 'chasers. All good judges are agreed that Golden Miller looks better than ever this year, though such appearances can be deceptive. He has not done anything to add to his reputation at the time of writing, but he has done all he has been asked to do, and he is, of course, a ready-made favourite for the National. Miss Dorothy Paget's eight-year-old gelding will be seen out at Cheltenham, when, in the race for the Gold Cup, we shall see whether he is the champion he was of old.

Above: Golden Miller, *one of the greatest steeplechasers of all time with five Cheltenham Gold Cups and a Grand National to his credit.*

DOROTHY PAGET

The name of Dorothy Paget became synonymous with *Golden Miller*. Many other words were also synonymous with the eccentric owner: spoilt little rich girl, man-hater, huge gambler. She was known to have been followed by a retinue of servants who when asked, which was frequently, had to provide meals in the middle of the night. Some trainers, of the highest calibre, were known to have to listen to her on the telephone all day. Indeed, Fulke Walwyn, as eminent a NH trainer as it is possible to get, once had to gesture for meals to be sent to him throughout an entire day while D.P. held court on the phone!

Dorothy Paget was born in 1905; her father, Almeric Paget, later Lord Queenborough, had been despatched to America with £5 and told not to come back until he had made his fortune. He did this by the simple expedient of marrying a rich heiress, Pauline Whitney, and the couple had two daughters, Olive (later Lady Baillie), and Dorothy. It was Dorothy, the younger, that Pauline doted on and spoilt. Dorothy discovered that by throwing a tantrum she could get whatever she wanted. When her mother died, Dorothy, at just twelve, became more self-willed and sullen than ever. It must have been a terrible shock for the petted, indulged darling, so perhaps it's no wonder that young Dorothy was expelled from every school she ever attended (six of them, the best that England could offer) until finally, at 'finishing school' in Paris she found a rapport with its owner, Princess Mestchersky, to such an extent that she even stayed there in the holidays; anything rather than be with her father, and reminded of the mother she adored. In time the Russian princess's sister, Madame Orloff, became her lifetime companion. These strong friendships were no doubt instrumental in Dorothy Paget setting up a home in Paris for elderly refugees of the Russian revolution. This benevolence was unknown to the world at large.

Much has been written about D.P., a large amount of it derogatory.

Remembered as immensely fat and inordinately plain, D.P. had once been slim and a good rider to hounds and of show horses. She was also an accomplished singer and a car-racing fanatic, taking the wheel herself, before her passion turned to racehorses.

Where or how she 'went wrong' is hard to pinpoint and in fairness, she appears to have been happy with the course she chose and with her way of life. More importantly, there are those who remember how amusing she could be and, behind the scenes, she was the unsung benefactor to many worthy causes and people, in addition to the Russian care home.

Dan Moore rode some horses for her in Ireland and found her good company and not without a joke when they met. She also owned Ballymacoll stud near Dunboyne in Co. Meath, which was managed by Charlie Rogers, part of another Irish racing dynasty. He also trained for her and was her racing manager from 1937 until her death in 1960.

She had a huge string of racehorses spread among a number of trainers, much the same as today's big owners; but if the whim took her, she would move them all without notice. At the time of her death Sir Gordon Richards was training some thirty for her on the Flat.

A number of trainers spoke highly and loyally of her, but many in the racing world derided her and blamed the downfall of her great chaser on her caprice. Unlike *Arkle* and *Best Mate*, *Golden Miller* did not have the good fortune to remain with one trainer throughout his racing life. But how much difference did it make? It is possible that the

Above: Gerry Wilson on Golden Miller *is led in by owner Miss Dorothy Paget after winning the 1934 Grand National.*

mighty *Golden Miller*, in true rich-boy fashion, was nearly as eccentric as his owner. He detested Aintree, (more precisely, he detested one particular fence where it is possible he got frightened), and refused to race there again – just as Dorothy Paget had hated school and refused to be educated. The Grand National brings out the best and the worst in horses, occasionally both; *Golden Miller* was one such. Some horses rise to the occasion and, winning or placed or even 'also ran' they continue year in and year out to put their best foot forward for the unique occasion. Others simply do not want to know, either straight off or after one experience. A good few previous winners have fallen at the first fence the following year. *Manifesto* and *Red Rum* were always superb. *L'Escargot*, trained by Dan Moore, hated it at first, but eventually adapted to the challenge.

GOLDEN MILLER

Golden Miller's promise turned into reality in his new ownership. After a couple of wins and places he won a three-mile chase at Gatwick in January 1932, at odds-on by a distance, and he was put by for his first assault on the Cheltenham Gold Cup. *Grakle*, the previous year's Grand National winner, was odds-on favourite and when he fell and brought down *Kinsford*, there were many who believed *Golden Miller's* victory was luck; certainly, it would have needed a crystal ball to predict that he would win four more.

He gained many more fans in the 1933 race with a clear victory and was installed favourite for his first attempt at the Grand National; it ended at the Canal Turn.

In the 1933–34 season *Golden Miller* and *Thomond II* met for the first time in early season races and both beat each other. Their epic duel was ahead of them, but *Thomond* did not run in the Gold Cup; *Golden Miller* had the 1934 race to himself, winning in a style that brought him many cheering fans acknowledging his three in a row.

And so to Aintree, with *Golden Miller*, looking a picture, second favourite. All the fancied horses were still in contention as they streamed over the water in front of the stands, and throughout the last circuit *Gregalach*, *Delaneige*, *Forbra*, *Thomond* and *Golden Miller* made a superb race of it. But once over the last fence it was *Golden Miller* who forged clear in a record time, putting five lengths between him and *Delaneige* with *Thomond* a further five lengths back.

Golden Miller's 1935 Gold Cup was supposed to be a 'pipe-opener' for the Grand National after facile wins earlier in the season. It was believed that *Thomond* was aiming for another race, but he, too, ran in the Gold Cup and one of racing's great duels ensued. From the downhill third last fence they had the race to themselves, neck and neck, stride for stride, the whole way. Jockeys Billy Speck on *Thomond* and Gerry Wilson on the *Miller* rode at the last as if it wasn't there, throwing caution to the wind. Both horses responded magnificently but gradually, inexorably up that final, famous hill, *Golden Miller* drew clear.

The magnificent chaser was now 2-1 for the Grand National, a race where just to get

Below: Tucker Geraghty erected a plaque on the stable where Golden Miller *was born, near Drumree in County Meath.*

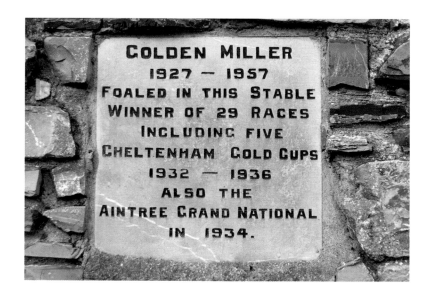

Above: Ross Geraghty at Fairyhouse, December 2007.

round should be at longer odds than that. But although he had won the year before, *Golden Miller* jumped poorly and slowly over the first three and by the time he reached the eleventh he cried enough. He barely took off and although he didn't actually fall his jockey, Gerry Wilson had no chance of staying in the saddle.

It was then that the human relationships slid downhill. It was decided that *Golden Miller* should run again the next day; it would seem the decision was Miss Paget's. This time the 'no' from the horse was even more emphatic – at the very first fence, and again his rider was dumped on to the turf. It led to a row between owner and trainer, resulting in D.P. removing all her horses forthwith; but it appears that it was Basil Briscoe who asked her to take them, not she who was dismissing him.

Gerry Wilson kept the ride a bit longer, but the following autumn, now trained by Owen Anthony, *Golden Miller* ran out at Newbury and the jockey was sacked. Replacing him in *Golden Miller's* fifth Gold Cup two weeks away was Evan Williams, a comparatively obscure jockey, but *Golden Miller* was back on his stage and galloped and fenced his way to his fifth Gold Cup.

Again he went to Aintree, but it was a similar debacle; knocked to the ground at the first fence, Evan Williams kept hold of the reins and remounted – but come the eleventh fence *Golden Miller* refused.

It seems extraordinary that he was tried again in the following year's Grand National, 1937 (different rider, same result: refused the eleventh). What was undoubtedly bad luck that year was the loss of Cheltenham to snow and with it *Golden Miller's* attempt on a sixth crown.

In 1938, aged eleven and ridden by 'Frenchie' Nicholson, he was second to a young pretender, *Morse Code*, the only time he was beaten at Cheltenham. It was an honourable defeat, and Cheltenham is rightly the place where he is remembered; he was retired after one more run the following February.

Dorothy Paget was a highly knowledgeable racehorse owner and, in later years breeder; the form, betting and welfare of her horses was a passion. When she lost thousands – tens of thousands – betting she forgot it, when she won she was delighted. The last of her record-breaking 1,532 winners came at Naas, Co. Kildare in January, 1960. She died at her home, aged fifty-four in February, 1960.

Golden Miller died three years earlier, aged thirty. In his retirement on her stud at Stanstead, Essex, with other companions, D.P. paid him regular visits, and ensured there were routine veterinary checks – and a supply of apples.

Above: The Geraghty siblings Barry, Jill and Ross before the Pinnacle Handicap Hurdle, Wexford, March 2007.

THE GERAGHTY FAMILY

Lawrence junior's son, Thomas, known universally as Tucker, continued the tradition of the family farm, a couple of hunters and one or two brood mares. He and his two brothers and three sisters all rode the family pony and enjoyed a little hunting. Tucker rode in a few point-to-points and would have loved to do more. Opportunities were limited, however, and he determined to provide more chances for his six children as they came along. He and his wife, Bea, hit upon the idea that was to provide the means for them if they wanted it. It was during the last downturn, in the 1980s. As part of farm diversification they opened a riding school that has steadily grown and gained a fine reputation. He also trains about half a dozen racehorses.

It meant that as Ross, Norman and Barry, Sascha, Jill and Holly were growing up they had the pick of any number of ponies to ride, go hunting on, to compete in Pony Club events – and to school and 'make' youngsters. What's more, the lads all worked hard at getting the business going.

The whole family loved hunting with the Ward Union in particular, and still do. All three sons began racing and the girls ride, too. Norman, a farrier to trainers Noel Meade and Tom Taaffe, is too heavy to be a professional, but is a successful amateur rider; Ross is a professional with an Irish Grand National under his belt; Jilly has won under NH rules as well as point-to-points; and Barry, always competitive as a Pony Clubber on a pony called *Vanity*, has become one of the world's leading steeplechase riders …

Barry's rise to the top was little short of meteoric: after riding his first winner in 1997 (at Down Royal for Noel Meade) he quickly caught the eye of other leading trainers, including Jessie Harrington for whom he won the Midlands Grand National in Uttoxeter that same season. Within two seasons he was crowned champion jockey of Ireland for the first time (1999-2000), and that was the year he began his incredible partnership with Jessie Harrington's *Moscow Flyer*; by the end of *Moscow's* career Barry had ridden him to twenty-four of his amazing twenty-seven wins. These famously included the Arkle Chase at Cheltenham, two 'Tingle Creeks' at Sandown and two 'Queen Mothers' for the two-mile Champion Chase, among a total of ten Grade Ones; in the early years it also included a pattern of falls/unseated riders.

Stars like *Florida Pearl* (Punchestown Heineken Gold Cup) and *Alexander Banquet* (Hennessy Cognac Gold Cup) proved Barry was not a one-horse wonder with *Moscow Flyer*. With *Kicking King* Barry won two 'King Georges' at Kempton on Boxing Day 2004 and 2005 as well as the 2005 Gold Cup. He was well and truly established as one of the most accomplished horsemen.

When the likes of *Kicking King* and, most recently, *Big Zeb*, came along to make monumental blunders (usually at the last fence), Barry has stuck his legs forward at take-off (when seeing that the stride was 'all wrong') and somehow lifted his mounts' noses up from off the ground on the landing side.

Barry's greatest spell in racing came in the spring of 2003, but the year before that had seen a special family occasion at the Irish Grand National of 2002. *Commanche Court*, trained by Ted Walsh and ridden by Ruby was favourite in spite of shouldering top weight of 12 stone, some 20lbs more than any other horse. This was following his Gold Cup second to *Best Mate*. Barry was on the second favourite, Dessie Hughes' *Rathbawn Prince*, who came next in the weights on 10.8. Among the lightweights was the horse ridden by his brother, Ross, still a 5lb-claimer, called *The Bunny Boiler*, one of two runners trained by Noel Meade.

As the three-mile five furlong event, held at Fairyhouse every Easter Monday, took shape, so *Commanche Court* pulled up and, at the third last fence, *Rathbawn Prince* fell. Ahead of him, as he started the lonely walk back, Barry could hear the roaring of the festive crowds, but he could neither see nor hear who the winner was. He asked a spectator and

Above: Barry Geraghty with his fiancée Paula Heaphy after winning the 2009 JCB Triumph Hurdle on Zaynar.

was told 'number seventeen.'

So, that must be a lightweight. Could it even be his brother? Yes, indeed, Ross had 'stepped out of his brother's shadow' and landed Ireland's most popular steeplechase!

The following spring was fairytale stuff. Barry rode no less than five winners at the Cheltenham Festival, including *Moscow Flyer* in the Queen Mother Champion Chase.

His proud family was there to see him crowned leading rider of the week, and they crowded into the unsaddling enclosure no less than eleven times, for apart from his wins, Barry was also placed in six races.

Could it honestly get any better than this?

Grand National day at Aintree saw the whole family ensconced in the Liverpool track, enjoying the festival atmosphere, maybe a little nervous for Barry as he headed out on *Monty's Pass*, trained in Cork by Jimmy Mangan, for the great race. Barry's previous three rides in it had produced a sixth and two falls – but hopes were high.

Tucker Geraghty managed to get himself into the stand reserved for trainers with runners in the race, and tucked himself into the furthest corner.

There had been a gamble on *Monty's Pass*, but all the same there were half a dozen or so horses at shorter prices. *Monty* had had a dress rehearsal over the fences when second in the previous year's Topham Chase. He liked the place and showed it now, jumping with springs in his heels, always handily placed, keeping out of trouble, ears pricked enjoying himself as he flew the formidable fences – and giving Barry a dream ride all the way to the winning post!

Up in the trainers' stand, stuck the far side, Tucker Geraghty scrambled his way through more like a prize fighter than the normally calm farmer and trainer. He met Holly at the bottom of the steps, tears streaming down, and they joined the rest of the family – coercing, cajoling, talking their way into the winner's enclosure; a day that dreams are made of.

The winners have kept coming for Barry and in 2008, following the retirement of Mick Fitzgerald, he landed the plum job of number one jockey to Nicky Henderson in Lambourn, England, commuting five days a week and riding in Ireland on the remaining two, *á la* Ruby Walsh.

He culminated the season with three superb Cheltenham Festival 2009 wins, the Irish Independent Arkle on *Forpadydeplasterer* for an enthusiastic Irish syndicate and Kerry trainer Tom Cooper; the JCB Triumph Hurdle on *Zaynar* and the Kappa Smurfit Champion Hurdle on *Punjabi* (both trained by Nicky Henderson), thus becoming the only jockey currently riding to have won the big four at Cheltenham (Kappa Smurfit Champion Hurdle, *Punjabi*, 2009; Four Seasons Queen Mother Champion Chase, *Moscow Flyer*, 2003 and 2005; Ladbrokes World Hurdle, *Iris's Gift*, 2004; Totesport Gold Cup, *Kicking King,* 2005) and the Martell Cognac Aintree Grand National (*Monty's Pass*, 2003).

2009 is the year in which Barry will be thirty, and in January 2010 he plans to marry Paula Heaphy, mother of their three-year-old daughter Síofra, a second grandchild for Tucker and Bea; Norman is married to Shona McDonogh, sister of the top Flat jockey, Declan, and they have a son, Charlie.

WHAT ODDS

No matter what the success, daily life remains a family affair with the Geraghtys, and the phrase 'family horse' takes on a new dimension with *What Odds*.

The now retired thirteen-year-old by *Torus* is owned by Mrs Bea Geraghty, was bred and trained by Tucker, and four of their children have won races on him. He was a six-year-old before he first ran, in a point-to-point behind *Hi Cloy* who went on to be a multiple Grade One winner for Michael Hourigan. After that, ridden by Norman Geraghty, he won his next point-to-point by twenty lengths and went on to make it four wins in a row, from spring 2002 through to January 2003.

Through Barry's connection in riding *Monty's Pass* for Mike Futter, he introduced the flamboyant owner to Tucker and a deal was done – which included the horse remaining in the Meath yard.

In thirty-five runs on the track the bay gelding has been ridden in all but five of them by a Geraghty. Back in the early days, when he won the Champion Hunter Chase at the

2003 Punchestown Festival, he was ridden by W.F. Codd because Norman, his regular point-to-point rider, could not do the weight.

His first race of the next NH season, in November 2003, he won his first handicap chase in the hands of Ross Geraghty in Fairyhouse, and he remained his most regular rider, though Barry also rode him a number of times, winning the January 2005 Grand National Trial at Punchestown on him.

The game horse was running in many of the country's leading handicaps and in England: Cork National, Kerry National, Ulster National, the Eider Chase at Newcastle, the Becher Chase at Aintree, a Cheltenham Festival handicap, that sort of thing; he also ran in the Irish National three times; but the handicapper and age were catching up with him and it was harder to win races.

It looked as if Barry's win in the National trial might be the last, especially when he 'got a bit of a leg' after running a cracking race in the La Touche cross country race in Punchestown 06.

He was pin-fired and rested for a year and a half, at which time Mike Futter gave him to the Geraghtys. When *What Odds* returned it was to give a first ride in a point-to-point to Jill Geraghty; before long she, and occasionally Ross, rode him under Rules again.

It was at the Fairyhouse Easter Festival in March 2008 that the Geraghty family had one of their brightest days. *What Odds*, now twelve years old, was priced at 33-1 in the Menolly Homes Handicap Chase. But the game horse knew nothing of that and he set off to make all the running, jumping superbly; the hot favourite, *Hold The Pin* from Tony Martin's stable, almost closed with him at the last fence, but jumped left. *What Odds* lived up to his name as the outsider ran on gallantly to beat the favourite in a field of eighteen rivals that included both Jill's professional brothers; Ross was fifth on *Aghawonan* and Barry pulled up on *Ballyfinney*.

Although now officially retired, *What Odds* just could come out again to act as a schoolmaster to another Geraghty, Holly, in a point-to-point.

The whole family supports each other; Barry's brothers and sisters root for him in the big time, and he in turn loves nothing more than to see any of them win.

Happy days indeed.

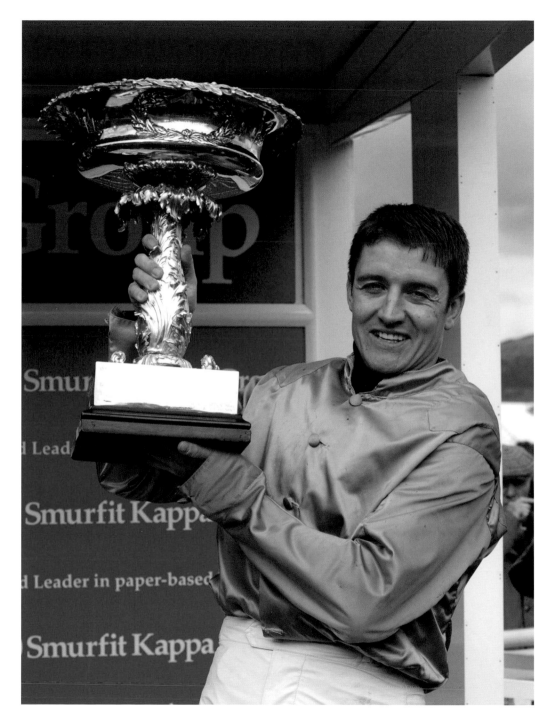

Above: The pinnacle of a memorable 2009 at Cheltenham: victory in the Smurfit Kappa Champion Hurdle on Punjabi.

Above: Happy couple: Ruby Walsh greets his wife Gillian after his 2009 Cheltenham Gold Cup win on Kauto Star.

FROM CORK TO KILL
VIA AMERICA – THE WALSHES

CHELTENHAM NATIONAL HUNT FESTIVAL, MARCH 2009: *Quevega. Mikael D'Haguenet. Cooldine. Master Minded. Big Buck's. American Trilogy. Kauto Star.* Seven winners, all ridden by Ruby Walsh.

Punchestown National Hunt Festival, April 2009: *Hurricane Fly. Master Minded. J'Y Vole. Jayo. Jessies Dream. Fiveforthree. Ballytrim. Equus Maximus. Mikael D'Haguenet. Sesenta.* Ten winners, all ridden by Ruby Walsh.

This is the bare bones, for the record. A record that is likely to remain for aeons.

The Kaiser Chiefs song 'Ruby, Ruby, Ruby, Ruby' has become linked to him by the media, often sung by fans as he rides into a winner's enclosure; a song, 'The Ballad of Ruby Walsh', has been written especially for him by Irish folk singer Christy Moore.

Ruby is at the top of the game. And Cheltenham and Punchestown 2009 were virtually on another planet.

Yet it so nearly might not have happened. The fall the previous November in Cheltenham seemed innocuous enough and Ruby walked to the ambulance, telling himself that if he could do that he must be OK, attempting to ignore the pain in his stomach, willing it to go away.

But within no time Ruby was undergoing surgery to have his spleen removed. He spent the next six days in hospital. Exactly three weeks after being discharged, he was back riding – white-faced, but as dynamic in the saddle as ever, simply getting on with the job he loves.

That he was able to return at all that season was one thing, to end it as he did was nearly unbelievable: not only leading rider at both Cheltenham and Punchestown, but also leading rider in Ireland – and he spends five days a week riding in England! It was his seventh Irish title, the last five of them won consecutively.

His father Ted Walsh, the former record-breaking Irish amateur turned racing TV presenter and trainer, rode a commendable four NH Festival winners at Cheltenham spanning his amateur career, including one of the Big Three. To watch his professional son win seven at one Cheltenham Festival, including the Gold Cup itself, was something else again – until, that is, six short weeks later, and Ruby comes up with an astonishing ten at the Punchestown Festival.

Ted Walsh's face said it all. Part of the art of a commentator is not to show bias towards

Below: Ted Walsh in RTÉ action at Fairyhouse, Easter 2009.
Overleaf: Brendan Sheridan, who spent his riding life with the Walsh family, seen here winning the 1988 Irish Grand National on Perris Valley *(trained by Dermot Weld).*

a loved one during a race – be they winning or being stretchered off – and Ted Walsh remains professional whenever he is speaking on air. But camera shots of him when off air watching Ruby speak volumes. Ted is seldom at a loss for words and verbosity is something of a trademark, but Ruby's records at National Hunt Racing's two principal Festivals produced not only delightfully open smiles from the jockey – as big for the last winner as for the first – but also from Ted and the rest of the family. It is the same when his daughter Katie rides a winner. Joining in with the smiles at Punchestown were Ted's wife, Helen, and their older daughter, Jennifer. Out manning her jewellery trade-stand somewhere among the throngs of visitors was Ruby's wife, Gillian. And his rugby playing brother, Ted junior, is there among his supporters, too. It is a family affair.

Having survived the spleen operation, Ruby's 2009 Cheltenham Festival still nearly ended before it began when he took a crashing fall with the favourite, *Tatenen*, at the third fence of the meeting's second race. Yet there he was, riding in the next race (fourth), and the next, second on *Celestial Halo* in the Champion Hurdle to his countryman Barry Geraghty on *Punjabi*. He sat out the cross-country race (won by Nina Carberry) and then won the last impressively, the David Nicholson Mares' Hurdle, on *Quevega*. *Quevega* is a small mare with a big heart and she 'bolted in'. Ruby was on the scoreboard.

Next day, the Wednesday, brought a brilliant treble in all three Grade 1 events, and all three of them started favourite. For the Ballymore Novices' Hurdle it was *Mikael D'Haguenet*, followed by *Cooldine* in the RSA Chase, both of these for Willie Mullins.

Next up was the Queen Mother Champion Chase for which the undefeated odds-on *Master Minded* was bidding to defend his crown. He jumped superbly and ran out a convincing winner beating the horse who was probably the training feat of the meeting, David Pipe's *Well Chief*, who had been off the course for two years.

Since Cheltenham became a four-day Festival in 2005, the Thursday feature has become the World Hurdle over three miles, and this produced Ruby's only winner for the day, *Big Buck's*, in a rousing finish against Barry Geraghty on *Punchestowns*.

Friday, the fourth and final day, brings steeplechasing's most treasured crown, the Cheltenham Gold Cup. But before that the crowds were treated to the rare sight of Ruby winning on a 20-1 outsider, *American Trilogy* in the Vincent O'Brien Handicap Hurdle.

For the Gold Cup, the NH world was divided between stable-mates *Denman* and *Kauto Star*. Other good horses were in it as well, of course, with a competitive field of sixteen making the line up. But the notion of stable companions who lived harmoniously side-side-by-side and competed fiercely on the race track had caught the public imagination. It was all about the big two: *Kauto Star* the nippy, athletic winner of 2007; *Denman* the huge, long-

Above: Down to business – Ruby and his agent, his sister Jennifer, discuss plans.

striding chaser whose win over his stable companion in 2008 was so impressive that viewers felt they had seen the winner for a few more years to come. *Denman* was awesome that day, but Ruby didn't lose faith with *Kauto Star*, as 2009 demonstrated.

In the intervening year *Denman* had suffered a heart problem; it was touch and go whether he would make it to the start at all and Paul Nicholls and his team did brilliantly to get him there.

The year before, Ruby had stuck with *Kauto Star*, to almost inevitable snide remarks from those grandstand jockeys talking afterwards with the benefit of hindsight. Ruby sided with him again in 2009.

And again the finish concerned the two horses who are not only in the same trainer's Somerset yard, but who also happen to occupy adjacent stables.

This time it was all about *Kauto*, although *Denman* ran gallantly considering the tribulations he had suffered. *Kauto Star's* victory was the first time a former holder had ever won back the crown after having lost it.

With this success Ruby had secured a record breaking seven Festival winners including three of the four principal races. The abiding image is of the look of sheer love and human happiness between Ruby and his wife as he went to weigh in after *Kauto Star*.

Channel 4's *Morning Line* is a part of many race-goers' Saturday breakfast fare, with regulars such as Johnny Francome, John McCririck, Alastair Down, Lesley Graham, Jim McGrath, Tanya Stephenson, Derek Thompson and Co. At 8am on Saturday 25 April 2009, Ruby Walsh is their guest, neatly dressed in a pin-striped suit, looking ahead to Punchestown and reflecting on his glorious Cheltenham.

'I don't tire of looking at the pictures from Cheltenham,' he says, 'it was a great week and the Gold Cup was the highlight, a special day. A lot of work went on in the stable and they pulled it off really well.

'*Kauto* felt like he did the first year, winning the Tingle Creek and 'King George' with raw speed and pace. Last year [when he was beaten in the Gold Cup] I was hoping the others would slow down, this year it didn't matter.'

When asked about injuries, he says, 'You hope you're going to be OK in five minutes.'

The panel remarked that where an office worker would be out for six months after the loss of a spleen, he was back in twenty-seven days.

Johnny asks him how he manages to be on the right horse most of the time.

'It's a balancing act,' says Ruby, 'the more people you ask the more clouded it becomes so I just have to go with my choice. I can only ride one so I go with the one who I think has the best chance.'

He praised his agent, his sister Jennifer: 'She's brilliant.'

The panel commended Jennifer for President – or, they suggested, she should be 'out there negotiating in Iraq.'

Such is the esteem in which Jennifer is held!

Ruby said that if punters get angry when they lose money on him that is their problem.

'It doesn't affect me because I am riding for the trainer and owner; I know punters are needed to keep racing going, but it's not for me to worry if they lose.'

Had he known there had been a huge gamble on his father's horse, *Papillon*, for the 2000 Grand National?

'Of course I knew. But winning the National for Dad was the best day.'

Ruby is always open, honest, frank; polite, charming, and (usually) tolerant, but what he lives for is race-riding.

On the opening day of Ireland's NH Festival at Punchestown 2009, the first race, over the cross-country course, was brilliantly won by Katie Walsh riding *Wedger Pardy*, trained by her father. The second, more predictably, was won by Ruby (*Hurricane Fly* in the Champion Novice Hurdle). Afterwards, the big screen quoting prices for the meeting's leading jockey read Miss K. Walsh 100-1; R. Walsh 1-2 …

Later in the week, Katie rode *Wedger* again, in another cross-country race. That she did well to get him back into the race when carried off the course by a loose horse towards the end was well noted; what few noticed was how nearly she was knocked out of the saddle in an early fence collision. Using gymnastic feats she got back into the saddle – and then took the lead, seemingly out of harm's way, until the loose horse interfered; they did well to finish fourth.

Ruby, meanwhile, had won the Champion Steeplechase on *Master Minded*, but only just, from *Big Zeb* who had blundered at the last. More winners rolled in and after the success on *Ballytrim* in Friday's 24-runner 3m6f marathon handicap chase he confessed, 'When Jennifer rang me yesterday and said I was riding him I wasn't exactly pleased, I didn't think he would like the mud, but he just kept on.'

In the next race, a 2m5f handicap chase, nearly all the twelve runners are together two out, but by the line he and *Equus Maximus* have put four lengths between them and their nearest pursuer. Ruby continues to smile, the bookies less so.

There is another great win to come that day when *Mikael D'Haguenet* holds off his stable companion *Cousin Vinny* (Patrick Mullins) in the 2½ -mile Land Rover Champion Novice Hurdle in a much talked about duel. Hopes had always been high for *Vinny's* prospects and he had been working 'out of his skin', but *Mikael* has been the revelation of the season, Willie tells viewers.

Ruby rides one final Festival winner on the Saturday – on the diminutive *Sesenta* – in his 'unbelievable week'. The filly is an 'absolute pony, probably the smallest I've ever ridden,' Ruby says, who then receives various accolades for the meeting and for the year, smiling as always, before setting off to watch the 'great lads' in the Leinster/Munster semi-final of the Heineken Cup at Croke Park.

'They're great ambassadors for the country,' he says. Just as Ruby and his colleagues are.

Like many other racing dynasties the Walshes are a close-knit family and all are involved in NH racing, even if only to support. Ted is the ever popular RTÉ Television racing presenter (along with Robert Hall) and trains a number as well; Ruby is first jockey to Paul Nicholls in England and to Willie Mullins in Ireland; and sorting and juggling his rides is his agent, his other sister Jennifer; she also helps her father on televised racing days by escorting winners and others to the interview box.

Above: Ruby and his sister Katie both rode winners on the opening day of the 2006 Punchestown Festival – and repeated the process in 2009.

THE OLDER GENERATION

It all began with Ruby senior (he was christened Edward, but nicknamed Ruby because of his golden, curly hair) down in Co. Cork in a town called Kildorrery on the Mitchelstown to Mallow road. Ruby was the youngest of nine children: Michael (Mickey), Jim, Tommy, Ted, Madge, Mary, Sheila, Pat and Edward (Ruby). In his earlier years, Ruby managed the family pub and also kept a few horses on the family farm at the bottom of

Above: Ruby Walsh senior, widely respected in the Irish racing world. In his early years he was also a Cork hurler.

the town near the River Funcheon.

Kildorrery is built on a cross-roads on an ancient hill fort site between the Ballyhoura Mountains and the Nagle Mountains, and neighbours the parish of Doneraile, finishing point of the first recorded steeplechase from Buttevant in 1752.

A 'black ditch' forms one boundary of Kildorrery dating back to 200 BC; and Brian Ború's brother, Mahon, is said to have been killed in the pass of Redchair, north of the village.

The present town was built in the early nineteenth century by Lord Kingston of Mitchelstown and it is said that when Lord Doneraile threatened to burn it down 'because it was a nest of sedition', Lord Kingston replied, 'If you burn Kildorrery today, I will burn Doneraile tomorrow.'

Local legends and stories celebrate eccentric characters from all strata of the social scale; during the 1930s the town's landlords used to give a pint of porter to Paddy the peddler, a lone beggar who visited the town biannually. He slept in the ruined mill on the River Funcheon where once 1,200 stacks of flour a year had been milled. One night Paddy fell into the river on his return from the pub and drowned; his faithful dog was taken in by a Kildorrery family. At the other end of the social scale was author Elizabeth Bowen of Bowen's Court House, now demolished; her novels were based on the Kildorrery area and 'the big house'. The memorial plaque to her in nearby Farrahy Church reads, 'She left in her writings a proof of her genius, a reflection of her personality and a history of her home.'

So it was in this part of north Cork, steeped in the tradition of steeplechasing and GAA, that Ruby Walsh plied his trade: farming, keeping a horse or two, and managing the pub. He hunted with the Duhallow and enjoyed point-to-pointing, but his forte was in buying and selling, and one of his most lucrative deals was brokering the regular supply of troop horses.

Two of Ruby's brothers emigrated to America; Michael (Mickey) Walsh who became a famous steeplechase trainer departed in 1925. He was followed by Jim who ran a riding school at Great Neck on Long Island. He owned and ran it with Mickey at the beginning but Mickey moved on from it at a later stage.

Mickey made quite a name for himself in North Carolina as seen in the picture of him jumping bareback and without a bridle (and needless to say, no hard hat) over a 6ft 1in timber fence; his seat and balance is perfect – talk about horsemanship being in the blood! Mickey was the founder of Stoneybrook Farm race track in Southern Pines, North Carolina.

Jim's son, Tommy, became a famous jockey who won the American Grand National several times. He was inaugurated to the Hall of Fame a few years ago, and is still alive today. He is a first cousin of Tom Walsh, who runs the pub in Kildorrery, and of Ted Walsh.

When Ted Walsh was barely more than a toddler his parents, Ruby and Helen, lured by these glowing reports from the other side of the Atlantic, set sail for a new life there, as a result of which another of Ruby's brothers, Tom, took over the running of the pub and the farm in Kildorrery where both businesses still thrive today.

Walsh's Corner House occupies a prime position on the crossroads in the town centre; it is run by Tom's son, Tom and his wife Noreen, and their son, Tom, the fourth generation Walsh to do so. Tom and Noreen have three more sons, Austin, Brendan (who is a farrier), and Michael.

They continue the Cork tradition not only of breeding and running a few horses, but

Below: Rightly proud mum Helen Walsh with Ruby, Cheltenham 2008.

also of being Cork GAA players.

Austin, married in the summer of 2009, has five All-Ireland hurling medals to his name; the original Ruby, Ted Walsh's father, was also a Cork hurler.

Tom and Noreen breed NH horses and among the photographs in the pub is one of Tom flanked by Henrietta Knight and Terry Biddlecome at the local point-to-point in Kildorrery. Another picture is of the fine NH mare the home-bred, *Function Dream*, who won eleven chases, including, after she moved to England for trainer Mary Reveley, the Victor Chandler at Ascot and the Game Spirit at Newbury.

She was all set to run in the Queen Mother Champion Chase in 2001 – Tom and Noreen already had their tickets booked – when the whole meeting was abandoned due to the disastrous foot and mouth epidemic.

The family connection with America is still strong and in 2005 Austin and Donna Walsh, and Ted and Helen Walsh, travelled over to Belmont to watch *Artie Schiller* win the Breeders Cup Mile, (Turf). *Artie* is owned by Mickey's grandson Thomas J. (Tom) Walsh and his wife Denise Entemann, of North Carolina. In a twenty-two-race career *Artie Schiller* won ten races and finished in the first four in all bar one of the remainder. The bay by *El Prado* now stands at stud in Kentucky.

Below: The remarkable Walsh family – Michael Walsh (Ted's uncle) riding without bridle or saddle over a 6ft 1in fence in America in 1940; like all the family, good hands, good seat, great balance.

His owners, Thomas and Denise, have a second home in Kildorrery and visit for extended periods up to three or four times every year. Naturally they follow the successes of Ruby junior and the rest of the family with pride.

For their part, Ted and Ruby brought *Papillon* down to Kildorrery to parade after his Grand National win in 2000.

So the American connection remains strong with the Walsh family, but it was not the life for Ruby senior and his family. They didn't like it, couldn't settle – for one thing they found the winters bitterly cold – and after only a few short years, moving between North Carolina, Belmont and Saratoga, they returned to Ireland, this time to the Phoenix Park in Dublin. Ruby set about training more seriously and in 1960 the family moved for the final time, to Kill, in Co. Kildare, close to Naas.

There Ruby continued to train until his death in 1990, and it was where a twenty-five-year association with the family began for Brendan Sheridan, now a Turf Club official.

He was walking home from school past the stables one day, aged ten, and asked Ruby if he could ride. He was put up on a pony called *Midge* from whom he had many falls while learning to ride – but he became Ruby's stable jockey, joining the staff as soon as he left school. He never worked in another yard and is fulsome in his praise of the whole family.

'Ruby was a true gentleman in all aspects of life, around the yard or when racing; he and his wife were both very good to me.'

The horse that got him going as a jockey was *Barney Burnett*, and another was *Golden Frieze* on whom he won five or six races before the horse was sold to Jenny Pitman's yard. Brendan also won the Triumph Hurdle at the Cheltenham Festival on *Rare Holiday* for Dermot Weld and the Irish Grand National on *Perris Valley*, also for Dermot Weld.

Brendan's first winner was in Tramore which was also the venue of his last winning ride. He broke in *Papillon*, and rode him to his first win on his debut in a maiden hurdle in Punchestown in February 1996 – an extraordinary race in which ten of the twenty runners took the wrong course! And Brendan was there when all of Ted and Helen's children were born.

When Ted, the leading amateur rider, took over the licence following his father's death, Brendan rode his first winner, *Rock The Prince*, in the Thyestes Chase, no less.

'I'm proud to have been associated with the whole family,' Brendan says, 'I can't speak too highly of them.'

Of those that Ted has trained, the principals are probably *Commanche Court*, *Rince Ri*, *Papillon* and *Jack High*.

Papillon memorably won the 2000 Aintree Grand National, the second successive Irish father/son, trainer/rider combination to do so, following *Bobbyjo* for Tommy and Paul Carberry in 1999.

Also in 2000 the Ted Walsh-trained and Ruby Walsh-ridden *Commanche Court* won the Irish Grand National and the Punchestown Gold Cup. He also won the 1997 Triumph Hurdle among a total of eleven wins, and ran *Best Mate* to two lengths in a Gold Cup. This popular horse died in May 2009.

Rince Ri ran every season from 1997 until 2006, since when he continues to do sterling work as a schoolmaster at RACE. Among his twelve wins were the Ericsson Chase at Leopardstown twice and the Bobbyjo Chase at Fairyhouse.

One of Ruby Walsh senior's proudest moments came in 1979 when Ted won the Queen Mother Champion Chase on Mr. J. Sweeney's *Hilly Way*. Today it is the turn of Ted and Helen to feel parental pride at the numerous successes of Ruby, of the talent of their daughter, Katie, and of the support of all the family.

Right: Austin Walsh outside the pub in Kildorrery, Co. Cork, where Ruby Walsh senior spent his earliest years.

DREAPER DREAMS

10

Had it not been for World War II, *Prince Regent* would, in all likelihood, have won a string of Cheltenham Gold Cups. However, but for the war, Tom Dreaper would not have trained him.

Thomas William (T.W. / Tom) Dreaper was born in 1898 and was a farmer's son. Not only did his father have no interest in racing, but he actively dissuaded his son from going into it.

The young Tom was surrounded by friends embroiled in hunting, point-to-pointing and racing. The more his father said 'no', the more Tom determined to follow that route. In 1923, when he was twenty-five, he moved away from home and set about farming from Greenogue, a good-sized farmhouse and mixed farm near Killsallaghan on the borders of Counties Dublin and Meath. Before long he was cutting a dash behind hounds with the Ward Union staghounds, keeping up with the best of them. From there he progressed to point-to-pointing even if, to begin with, his first 'paying guest' was tucked away out of his father's sight at the far end of the farm. He set about training for his first patron, one T.H.

DREAPER DREAMS   165

Above: Arkle *in box 7 at Greenogue with trainer Tom Dreaper, daughter Valerie, and Sputnik the terrier.*
Opposite bottom: Trainer Jim Dreaper at Fairyhouse on a cloudless January day, 2009.
Overleaf: Punchestown 2009 and Notre Pere *and Andrew Lynch clear the last to win the Guinness Gold Cup for trainer Jim Dreaper and owners Mr and Mrs P.J. Conway.*

(Henry) Baker of Malahow. In later years his widow, Alison, was to breed *Arkle*. Although Mr Baker did not live to see *Arkle*, he did enjoy success via Tom Dreaper with both *Arkle's* dam and grand-dam, *Bright Cherry* and *Greenogue Princess*. Tom himself won the Fingal Harriers point-to-point on *Greenogue Princess*, achieving his long-held ambition, and the mare went on to breed no less than twelve winners, including *Arkle's* dam, *Bright Cherry*. *Bright Cherry*, in turn, showed a lot of speed and won a hurdle race and six chases, and was placed a further eleven times.

Within a few years of Tom Dreaper's one-horse beginnings the racehorse side of things was proving more successful than the farming. He caught the eye of J.V. (Jimmy) Rank in England who had his young horses broken and prepared for racing by Paddy Power in Waterford. Tragically, Paddy Power was killed in a car crash *en route* to the Dublin Horse Show. The batch of four youngsters was transferred to Tom Dreaper; the year was 1938. The deal was that when they were ready for the track they would return to England to race –

but the following year saw the outbreak of World War II, followed by the cessation of racing in Britain. The original group of youngsters were returned to Tom Dreaper, to begin their racing careers in Ireland. It was the start of a long association between owner and trainer.

Even more significant is that one of those first horses was named *Prince Regent*; Tom Dreaper rode him to win a flat race in Naas, and in 1942, ridden by Tim Hyde, he won the first of Tom Dreaper's ten Irish Grand Nationals. It was not until 1946, after the war, that the strapping chaser, standing 17hh, could travel to England where, at the age of eleven, he won the Cheltenham Gold Cup and was third, carrying a huge weight, in the Grand National, giving two stone to most of his opponents. He won eighteen races and placed thirteen times from forty-five starts, and it was well into *Arkle's* career before Tom could believe *Arkle* was better than his *Prince*.

By now quiet, pipe-smoking Tom Dreaper with his wry smile had emerged as a top trainer. In 1945 he had married Elizabeth Dreaper, known as Betty. She was a tall, slim, educated, elegant lady, who also rode brilliantly to hounds. The couple had three children, Eva, who married Flat trainer Michael Kauntze, Jim and Valerie. Mr Rank was godfather to Jim.

In the ensuing years Betty handled the paper work, the press, and scores of random visitors with aplomb – and a smile. As Tom's health became frail, she frequently represented him at the races in England. In later years, as a widow, she married one of their owners, Sir John Rogerson, and lived in the Cotswolds not far from Cheltenham, scene of so many triumphs and memories. As well as memories, there were continuing successes, as her son, Jim, became a regular trainer there, too.

Above: Fairyhouse 2005, Jim Dreaper with his son, Tom.

Arkle memorably won three Gold Cups and a Broadway at Cheltenham in the mid 1960s; those lucky enough to have seen him live remain convinced that he was the best steeplechaser ever; but before that Tom Dreaper horses had already secured many victories at the Gloucestershire home of NH racing. *Fortria* twice won the Mackeson Gold Cup in the early 60s, and the 1960 and 1961 Two Mile ('Queen Mother') Champion Chase, a race in which Tom Dreaper still has the best record of any trainer. After *Fortria* he won it with *Ben Stack* (1964), *Flyingbolt* (1966), *Muir* (1969), and *Straight Fort* (1970).

Tom Dreaper was always renowned for bringing on 'old fashioned chaser types'; it went without saying that they were Irish-bred. He was patient with them, never over-galloped them, but always had them well-schooled, qualities that were passed on to his son.

After a successful amateur riding career that saw Jim tantalisingly close to winning the Aintree Grand National (on *Black Secret*, an agonising neck second to *Specify*), Jim himself trained the Gold Cup winner *Ten Up* in 1975 and the winners of four Irish Grand Nationals: *Colebridge* 1974 and *Brown Lad* in 1975, 1976 and 1978.

He and his wife, Patricia, have three children, Tom, an amateur rider who is now Jim's assistant trainer, Lindsay and Shona, who is marketing manager at Punchestown Racecourse.

Today Jim has a horse that looks straight out of the *Prince Regent* mould – with one exception. Like *Prince Regent*, *Notre Pere* stands 17 hands high, and is a lovely bay with deep girth, strong limbs, kind head and a great racing attitude – but he is French-bred, not Irish.

Like father, like son, Jim has been so patient with the out and out stayer who needs soft ground; if he doesn't get it, Jim withdraws him and waits some more.

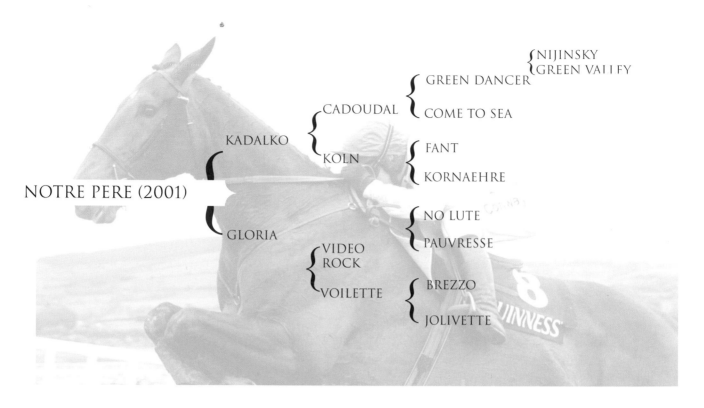

NOTRE PERE (2001)

KADALKO
- CADOUDAL
  - GREEN DANCER
    - NIJINSKY
    - GREEN VALLEY
  - COME TO SEA
- KOLN
  - FANT
  - KORNAEHRE

GLORIA
- VIDEO ROCK
  - NO LUTE
  - PAUVRESSE
- VOILETTE
  - BREZZO
  - JOLIVETTE

Luckily he also has 'old-fashioned' patient owners in the shape of Mr and Mrs P.J. Conway from Northern Ireland. The 'gentle giant' of a horse did not run until he was five, unlike the smaller, lighter and much more precocious French-breds more usually seen. The secret is that *Notre Pere* is in the French QPS, the equivalent of the 'half-bred' book.

The Conways have had horses with Jim throughout his career, buying them as young as possible and then being patient for as long as needed.

At Christmas 2008 *Notre Pere* became the first Irish-trained horse to win the Welsh National at Chepstow, having earlier won the Troytown Chase in Navan. He was withdrawn from the Cheltenham Gold Cup, the Grand National and likewise from the Irish National when the ground came up too quick.

It is not so much that he can't handle good ground, more that on the soft it slows his speedier rivals down while he keeps up his relentless gallop.

'If only there were some five-mile chases, he'd win them all,' Jim says ruefully. 'The only thing he's really quick at is eating!'

His patience yet again paid off at Punchestown, for the Festival's most valuable prize, the Guinness Gold Cup, run on rain-sodden ground in late April 2009. Half of the twelve runners came over from England. *Notre Pere*, looking a picture, was led round the paddock by Paula Whelan, 2008 Stable Lass of the Year, and he was ridden by his regular jockey Andrew Lynch.

Notre Pere simply drew away from the pack in the last mile, sploshing through the mud and galloped them in to the ground, giving a superb exhibition of jumping in the process to win by thirteen lengths.

Afterwards Andrew said, 'The pace was a bit slow at first and he jumps better when it's quicker, he can stand off them more.'

Jim felt beforehand that his horse was 'bang on' and admitted the rain helped. Asked of his future plans, Jim said immediately, 'The Gold Cup, of course. Twice. If it comes up soft.'

Once home, Jim said, 'In theory there should be no need to run him in a handicap again…' (ruling out both the Aintree and Irish Grand Nationals).

'We can aim for the sky, and settle for the horizon.'

Isn't that what horse-racing's all about?

Below: In December 2008 Notre Pere *became the first Irish-trained winner of the Coral Welsh National at Chepstow for trainer Jim Dreaper.*

RECORDING THE SPORT
FOR POSTERITY
– AND BETTING ON IT

RACING GETS INTO THE BLOOD OF MANY OTHERS BESIDES OWNERS, trainers, jockeys and, of course, the horses. Apart from 'armchair' punters and race-going enthusiasts, there are numerous Turf officials – and there are those who record the sport for posterity via pen or camera as well as those 'on the other side' – the bookmakers.

The enthusiasm and sheer pleasure of working (extremely hard and long hours) within the sport/industry they love is self evident when speaking to brothers Tony and Peter O'Hehir, father and son Liam and Pat Healy, and Brian Graham and his siblings.

Mention the name of a particular racehorse and the response among racing aficionados will differ: for some, they will immediately recall its breeding; others, the gambles; the name of the owner and/or trainer and rider; or a particular race. For a photographer it is likely to be pictures he or she has taken of the horse; and for a commentator it is its colours that spring to mind.

For someone like Tony O'Hehir most colours are indelibly ingrained; occasionally it can be tricky if a multiple owner like J.P. McManus has several runners in a race, distinguished only by different coloured caps.

'But the hardest is likely to be a big field, with many of the horses relatively unknown,' says Tony, 'they take a bit of extra homework.'

Many Irish sporting fans, not only of racing, will remember with awe and admiration the O'Hehir's father Michael (also known as Mícheál Ó hEithir) for, before embarking on a horserace commentary career, he was, and remained, the 'voice' of Gaelic games. The excitement and accuracy with which he delivered his broadcasts were unforgettable.

Michael was born and educated in Dublin, as were Tony and Peter, but Michael's father, Jim, was a Co. Clare man and in 1914 he trained his home county to win the All Ireland Hurling Final; he also became a GAA official, so Michael grew up with Gaelic Games as a part of his life.

While still at school, Michael wrote to Radio Éireann, the forerunner of RTÉ, asking

Below: RTÉ sports commentator Michael O'Hehir (also known as Mícheál Ó hEithir) in the commentary box at Croke Park, Dublin, in June 1984. Michael O'Hehir started his career as a radio commentator in 1938. He was a regular commentator at the Becher's Brook stretch of the Aintree Grand National.

to do a test commentary. He was allowed to try his hand for the last five minutes of the first half of a football league game between Wexford and Louth. The response was astonishing, his commentary so polished that he was immediately asked to undertake the whole of the second half.

His first full GAA commentary was in 1938, aged eighteen, on the All-Ireland Senior Football semi-final, Galway v Monaghan, in Mullingar; soon afterwards he gave up his engineering studies at UCD after one year to become a full time sports commentator. He never looked back and the memory of his voice and expertise is held in awe still.

In 1944 he added sports journalism to his repertoire, writing for Independent Newspapers; gradually he began reporting on racing as well as GAA, while continuing commentating not only for Radio Éireann, but also the BBC.

By the end of that decade he had also taken in horse-racing commentary, but a bigger, more prestigious appointment awaited him: with the founding in 1961 of Ireland's first national television station, Teleifís Éireann, Michael was appointed head of sports programmes. He continued doing his GAA commentaries and there was a time in the 1971 All Ireland Hurling final that one of the players was running in bare feet.

Michael broadcast, 'And the bare-footed wonder with the ball now.' The name of the wonder was Babs Keating, whose daughter Orla was to marry top Irish jockey Johnny Murtagh. Babs Keating became a renowned trainer of the Tipperary hurlers.

Fate led Michael O'Hehir to his biggest professional challenge; he was on holiday in New York with his wife Molly when the US President John F. Kennedy was shot dead in 1963. Teleifís Éireann contacted him and asked for a live commentary of the funeral, all five hours of it.

Although a totally different sphere to sport, his professionalism showed once again that he was a master at his art, and it led in later years to his giving the commentaries for the funeral of Roger Casement in 1965 and to the 1966 celebrations marking the fiftieth anniversary of the Easter Rising.

He became known to TV racing fans as being responsible for the stretch of Grand National from just before Becher's Brook until the horses were round the Canal Turn. He had already been commentating on the same stretch for radio for many years. It was from his eyrie above the fence after Becher's in 1967 that he gave a close up account of the huge pile up that resulted in the fence being named thereafter the 'Foinavon', of which more in a moment.

He was equally at home calling the horses on the Flat as he was over the jumps, probably the most famous two being *Shergar* and *Arkle*. He also commentated for show-jumping, including at Ireland's show-piece event the RDS in Ballsbridge, almost in the centre of Dublin city.

In 1972 he became manager of the re-vamped Leopardstown racecourse, but left a year later to turn freelance, which took him into American race coverage, including for the Arlington Million.

It was in 1985, just two weeks before he was due to commentate on his one hundredth All Ireland Final, that Michael suffered a stroke. He survived a further eleven years, but did not recover well enough to achieve his ambition of commentating on his hundredth. In 1987 there was an emotional tribute made in his honour before the start of that year's All Ireland Football final at Croke Park. The thousands of fans cheered him to the echo. He was a colossus among commentators.

NEW VOICES

It is hardly surprising, then, that sons Tony and Peter also became racing journalists and commentators, although Tony confesses to a brief time as a 'bolshy teenager', when so many people simply expected him to follow in his father's footsteps, that he vowed to be a teacher.

'But it didn't last long,' he confesses.

Tony's first recollection of going racing is watching a horse called *Tutto* win the Leopardstown Chase in 1957.

As a boy, when he was a pupil of the Marist Fathers' Chanel College, Dublin, Tony would assist his father with the Irish Form Book that he had started, helping with the indexing long before the computer age, and helping colour the Grand National colours on the cards.

Among his childhood memories is visiting the Galway races as part of the summer holidays the family spent with his grandparents in Co. Mayo: from 1957, when it was a two-day meeting, until the present, Tony has missed only one year at Galway.

He was a teenager when he accompanied his father to the 1967 Grand National at Aintree, stationed with him near Becher's Brook; it was at the following fence, the smallest on the course, that one of the biggest mêlées in the history of the race took place. A loose horse called *Popham Down* ran down the full length of the take off side in front of all the other horses, bringing down or baulking all the runners bar the backmarker, a 100-1 outsider called *Foinavon* …

'It was like watching a Western with the Indians being mowed down.'

Below: Like father, like sons, brothers Tony (left) and Peter O'Hehir (right) are also renowned commentators of the Irish Turf.

Above: All in a day's work for the commentator, calling home the action at Ballinrobe in 2008.

His father provided a slick, un-panicked and professional account that was his hallmark.

Tony's own first commentaries were for point-to-points, a good schooling ground, and from there he went on to his first racecourse commentary, a day etched indelibly on his memory. It was at Cork on an August Bank Holiday in 1969 so there were small fields, making commentary easier. Tony was nineteen years old and among the amateur riders that day was a 5lb claimer called Ted Walsh …

In the 1970s Tony became a regular on radio with occasional television stints, and he has been with RTÉ since 1981. Following his father's stroke in 1985, Tony became increasingly in demand. The next year, 1986, saw the launch of the *Racing Post* and he has been Irish correspondent for them ever since, a progression following the closure of the *Sunday Press*.

'It's a good team with strong rapport.'

He asked RTÉ to let him cover the 1993 Melbourne Cup, which for the first time had a European runner, Dermot Weld's *Vintage Crop*. They would not allow it, but did the following year, having missed the Irish win in 1993; his commentary came from the judge's box. Although the victory was not repeated then, the race has become a regular feature in Tony's *Racing Post* reportage and he often couples it with his annual holiday.

Among the Grand Nationals Tony has covered have been the void race of 1993 and the bomb scare year of 1997 when the whole course was evacuated. Tony was already down on his pitch at Becher's and had with him Brian O'Connor from the *Irish Times*, wishing to see the race from a different view. Instead, both had to walk into the centre of Liverpool and just managed to take the last two rooms in a hotel. No one, but no one, was allowed to either take their car or to return for their belongings in the Press Room. The re-run race on the Monday, won by *Lord Gyllene*, might have been lacking in atmosphere but all admired the racecourse for staging it.

The 2001 Grand National was an unforgettable day, but one that Tony wished he could. The rain poured continuously for twenty-four hours and the place was a quagmire; huge pools of water lay on the ground. A number of hacks claimed the meeting should be called off. But this was the year of foot and mouth, the spring when the Cheltenham NH Festival had had to be cancelled. The last thing racing needed was for Aintree to succumb. Safety was paramount, but the ground was so freshly wet – it didn't stop raining – that horses could slop their way through it and for fallers it was a soft landing.

And fallers aplenty there were.

Tony was, as ever, stationed at the Foinavon fence with his perfect view not only of that fence, but also of Becher's and the Canal Turn. (The commentary is divided between four broadcasters, each with his own traditional section to cover.) Horses had fallen at all of the first five fences, but as they approached the sixth, Becher's, the rain had got into the cables that should be about to relay Tony O'Hehir's voice. The sound technicians and engineers were there, but there was not enough time to solve the problem, hard as they struggled.

John Hanmer, getting no sound from Tony, filled in.

Tony says, 'It was very difficult for him, being far away in another corner of the course and having to operate off a monitor and poor pictures due to the driving rain.'

The leaders got over the Canal Turn, but then a loose horse careered across the remainder causing a ten-horse pile up. Tony's 'Foinavon' moment had arrived, the chance to emulate his father. It was not to be. The wires were still dead; there were no engineers on hand, there was nothing he could do. The depleted field continued on its way – six of Martin Pipe's record-breaking ten runners, a quarter of the field, were out by the seventh fence, and the field was down to single figures before they set out on the final circuit. In the end only *Red Marauder* and *Smarty* jumped round, slowly but clear. Two fences behind them, *Blowing Wind* and *Papillon*, Tony McCoy and Ruby Walsh, remounted to take third and fourth prize money.

'It was sickening for me,' Tony ruefully recalls, 'I might as well have stayed in bed, and it all happened so close to me that I wouldn't even have needed binoculars.'

Not long after, when Tony O'Hehir joined the English press for dinner in Cashel, Co. Tipperary, the night before Aidan O'Brien's annual Open Day, his entrance was greeted with sign language from his overseas colleagues, jokingly taking the mickey out of him.

Today, with Irish racing coverage considerably increased, there are four *Racing Post* journalists covering Ireland.

'We try and organise it so that we all work a five-day week,' says Tony, 'but that is not always possible at the big Festivals.'

Not only is there the extra work, but at those times Tony will be taken up as racecourse commentator – though spend half an hour with him and there will be several journalistic calls coming up on his mobile phone as well: a trainer ringing back with prospects for his horse, an editor wanting more words, or fewer as the case may be. Four hours before the first race of Punchestown, and the Press Room is already buzzing.

Tony can vaguely remember the same buzz of seeing *Arkle* live in Ireland; and later of recording the great clashes of *Monksfield* and *Sea Pigeon* and *Night Nurse*. He loves NH racing and the 'good' Flat races, and his first course commentary was for *Nijinsky's* Irish Derby.

'I shall never forget the huge roar as he came up the straight.'

Tony's younger brother, Peter, has – unsurprisingly – followed a similar route.

'I was always surrounded by it and loved it,' he says, 'my father lived for every moment of it. For us it is good to be getting a living out of something we enjoy.'

Peter has been racing correspondent for the *Irish Daily Mirror* for ten years, for whom he also ghost writes various columns for such as Michael Kinane, Barry Geraghty and, in the *Istabraq* days, Charlie Swan.

'When Michael won the 2009 2,000 Guineas I was cheering so much everyone thought I had money on the winner, *Sea The Stars,* but it was just that I was so pleased for him, he's a consummate professional.'

Peter also deputises for Dessie Scahill as course commentator when needed, such as when there are two Irish meetings in a day. He took over from Tony as editor of the *Irish*

Form Book, founded by their father, eleven years ago. He has the greatest admiration for the National Hunt boys: 'They have no notions about themselves regardless of how well they are doing.'

One of Peter's earliest racing memories is from those family holiday times in Galway.

'I was on top of the Corrib stand and the only way I could see anything was to peer round the concrete pillars.'

These days, of course, he gets 'the best view in the house.'

From a strictly watching point of view the memories that stand out most for him are *L'Escargot's* Aintree Grand National win and, at the same venue, the dead-heat between *Night Nurse* and *Monksfield* in the Templegate Hurdle.

He has lived in Naas for the last fifteen years with his wife, Margaret and sons Conor, sixteen, and thirteen-year-old Eoin. He has continued the family involvement in GAA and has coached the team that has included Conor from the under-eights up to minor; Eoin is also playing for his age group.

The O'Hehir tradition lives on with great enthusiasm.

A LIFE IN PICTURES

Liam Healy's mother died when he was three years old, as a result of which her children had to be 'farmed out'. Liam was taken in by a childless couple living a couple of doors away from his father, Paddy, in Convent Street, Listowel, in Co. Kerry. The name of the lady who reared him was Hanny Carey and one thing she loved was a little bet on the horses; she used to ask the young lad to place a shilling on for her in Moriarty's, the illegal betting shop. What fascinated young Liam there were all the newspaper pictures of racehorses on the wall and after a while Roddy Sullivan, the office worker, used to keep them for him.

Eventually the place closed and, as they couldn't afford to buy a newspaper, Liam used to go to the town dump and rummage for the papers from which he could cut out the racing pictures.

'Pictures are a passion, not the horses, and pictures of horses are the biggest passion,' he says. But one day his father said he spent too much time with them and burnt the lot.

Nothing could completely erase his passion for the pictures, though. Years passed, he grew up and married Joan, with whom he had four children, Pat, Lisa, Liam and Cathy, and continued his job as a mineral drinks salesman. One morning in bed he let out a big sigh and when she asked, he confessed to Joan that he hated his job; all he wanted to do was

Above: Probably Pat Healy's most famous photograph: Listowel, 22 September 1997, the first fence in the Patsy Byrne Beginners Chase in which nine of the sixteen runners fell, (L-R) McFepend & Ken Whelan (brown & orange), Angareb & Shay Barry (red, on ground), Ask The Butler & Conor O'Dwyer (yellow & purple), Combine Call & Tom Treacy (grey, red cap), Strong Boost & Jason Titley (green), Owenduff & Richard Dunwoody (yellow & red, finished race), Call Bob & Kieren Gaule (pink cap, finished race), Conna Bride Lady & Tom Rudd (light blue, behind K. Gaule), Clon Dalus & Liam Cusack (Orange), Boreen Lass & Adrian O'Shea (on ground, blue and red) and Dromkeen & Norman Williamson (blue & white).

take photographs. Photography had become his hobby and once a week he would be able to sneak away from his job to a race meeting; he got friendly with two amateur jockeys, Ted Walsh and Pat Casserley, and they encouraged him to go full time. It was a huge risk, especially with a growing family, but Joan gave him her blessing and backed him to the hilt.

'She was my rock,' he recalls.

But it wasn't as easy as that. There were photographers covering the Dublin tracks, but none at the country meetings, nevertheless the Turf Club refused to give him a licence.

Liam Healy had to go out and prove himself on the point-to-point circuit, a scene where he is still a regular.

'I think they wanted to establish that I was willing to put in the time and commitment,' he says, adding, 'there was one Turf Club official who supported me all the way, Max Fleming, he was a clerk at the major tracks. I have a great deal of time for him.'

Liam is now widely recognised as one of Ireland's top racing photographers. Listowel is a long, long way from the majority of tracks, but Liam has a rule that, no matter how far away the meeting he attends, he drives home that night.

Many a journey has been lightened by having a passenger with him, and numerous stories has he listened to on the way.

One friend often given a lift was the late Christy Costello who used to work for the course bookmakers throughout the southern region before their boards became modernised with lights flashing up the prices.

'Christy was one of the many characters I have travelled with,' Liam recalls, 'we passed many a happy hour and it made the road shorter.'

Dick Fitzsimons, an ex-army man, had some brilliant stories to tell, and another was Tommy Walker, a trainer, who regaled him with amusing pony racing tales.

'I'm sure some of my passengers' stories got embellished along the way, but they certainly made the time pass quicker.'

The business remains a family affair, but sadly without his bedrock, Joan, who died in 1987 aged just forty-three.

Both Liam's sons are photographers and one of his daughters, Cathy does the books. Liam's grandson, Kevin O'Carroll son of Lisa, is a leaving certificate student and has begun taking point-to-point photographs; he is the third generation of Healy Racing to do so.

Below: The Healy family of photographers. Liam Healy (senior) with his sons, (right to left) Pat and Liam junior, and his grandson Kevin (left).

For Pat there was never a doubt about what he wanted to do. He accompanied his father racing from an early age and confesses, 'The easy part is going racing and taking pictures. The hard part comes in the office!'

With the advent of digital photography, however, times have changed considerably.

'Digital has made it so much easier, the camera does much of the hard work,' Pat explains, 'I no longer have to use a light meter, or correct the aperture or speed; there's no need for a dark room, the machine does it all.'

But there's a down-side. Where he used to able to go out for a drink in the evening after racing at Cheltenham, and then have two solid days in the office once home developing films and so on, he is now a slave to the laptop.

Drinks have gone out of the window because after up to seven hours on the racetrack he now spends another seven, firstly in the Press Room until about 7pm downloading pictures on to his laptop and then after an hour's break for a meal he is likely to be working until 1am, scrutinising every individual photograph, saving and recording a huge number.

'It is essential to start the next day with a clean slate on the camera, that is the secret,' he explains. 'Cheltenham is the biggest meeting of the year with the most number of pictures taken.

'But the plus side is that if someone comes to me in five years time I can find the image they want in about thirty seconds.'

Pat's enthusiasm for his job is infectious and although it has taken him all round the world he admits, 'Listowel is closest to my heart.'

He is also a director of Listowel Racecourse, elected to the board in his mid-thirties and a role he takes responsibly.

'It shows me another side of the industry; Listowel Festival used to be a social occasion for me, but now because I'm involved I daren't get a sore head!'

The course has both good and bad memories for him professionally. Photography involves skill in setting up pictures and taking them at just the right moment, but in a fast moving sport like racing it also involves a degree of luck, being in the right place at the right time. He could be standing at fence two and the pile-up occurs at the one before or after; or he could be standing the 'wrong' side of a fence so that the eventual winner is obscured by another horse.

But there was a time in Listowel when it went spectacularly right, from a photographic point of view. It was the Patsy Byrne Beginners Chase 1997 and Pat stood at the first fence.

A nine-horse pile-up happened right beside him and his shot of it (p. 182) now adorns his Pat Cash Healy business card.

His other favourite picture is a head shot of *Dawn Run* and *Buck House* being shown the first fence before the famous match in 1986 (p. 50).

On the other side of the coin, when he was ten or eleven years old, his father was at the last fence wanting to picture a particular horse, *No Hill*, for its owner, Mr O'Callaghan; it was ridden by Ted Walsh and trained by his father Ruby Walsh. Pat was standing at the winning line with his camera.

It was one of those times that the horse was mainly obscured for Liam.

'Don't worry,' said young Pat, 'I got him on the line.'

So with promises to send it on to the owner, father and son returned to their darkroom. But when Pat opened his camera, there was no film in it.

It was an impressive lesson …

Pat loves the camaraderie of the racing scene especially among the jockeys, many of whom have become friends. Charlie Swan and Norman Williamson were best men at his wedding in 1994, when he married Mags Horgan. They have two children, Siún and Jack.

'The bad days are when a jockey gets hurt. Before the days of mobile phones there have been times when I have had to get to a land-line and ring the wife …'

Norman Williamson's career ended with a neck injury in Downpatrick. Pat drove him home to Meath, trying to keep him cheerful, but able to see for himself that it would be the end of race-riding for his friend.

Norman Williamson, Charlie Swan and Eddie O'Leary (brother to Ryanair's Michael), married three sisters, Janet, Carol and Wendy, daughters of Cashel, Co. Tipperary-based Timmy Hyde. The Hydes are another racing dynasty, not only in the bloodstock agency and stud world, but also in riding. Timmy's father, Tim, won the 1939 Aintree Grand National riding *Workman*.

Pat stays with former jockey and now Turf official Brendan Sheridan when he stays up for Punchestown (unlike his father who drives the three hours there and back daily); back in 1987, Brendan's wife, Ann-Marie, was another of the women he had to contact to tell that her husband was badly hurt.

'But the two occasions in 2003 when Kieran Kelly and Sean Cleary were killed were by far the worst, they put the whole thing into perspective.'

They were tragedies, three short months apart, one jumping, the other on the Flat, which shook the close-knit community of Irish racing to the core.

Of the highlights in his photographic career Pat says, 'All the big days are highlights. I'm now contracted to the *Irish Field* and I cover the Breeders Cup in America, the big Hong Kong meeting in December, all the Festivals and Classic races here and in England.

'When I was little I never even dreamed of going abroad – and as for dressing up for Royal Ascot, yes, I love it. There are people working in factories who would give their eye teeth for what I do.'

He doesn't find the seven days of Galway a marathon, no way; like everything else he loves it, but of course the beauty of Killarney and his home town of Listowel remain the closest to his heart.

There remains one little question: where does the 'Cash' come from in Pat Cash Healy? A family name, perhaps? There are many Cash's in the Irish horse world …

Although he never had race-riding aspirations, Pat used to ride out for Ruby Walsh senior, in the days when Cash Asmussen was the leading American Flat jockey.

One morning, after rather a heavy night with a lot of pints downed, Pat was late into the Walsh stables at Kill, near Naas, and the rest of the string had already headed out to the gallops. He quickly saddled up and, riding extremely short for an amateur, he caught them up.

As he arrived, Ted Walsh, one of the riders, called out, 'Here comes Cash f**king Asmussen!' Brendan Sheridan was another rider that morning, and through him the nickname stuck.

THE BOOKIES

There is one thing about racing that lifelong bookmaker Brian Graham loves more than anything else, and that is when his mother, Brenda, has a runner.

Only after that will he put *Dawn Run* for chasing, and *El Gran Senor* on the Flat at the top of his racing greats.

Brian, along with five of his six siblings, is a part of Belfast's Sean Graham bookmaking business that was founded by their late father, Sean. Sean's great-uncle Mat had a betting shop in Belfast, and Sean's father, John, started off working as a bookmaker on the greyhound tracks, Celtic Park and Dunmore, both now lost to Belfast development, so bookmaking had already been a part of the Graham family for two generations before Sean set up the Sean Graham business.

It wasn't all plain sailing. When Sean began in the 1960s he was unable to obtain a licence in southern Ireland, where almost all of the horse-racing tracks are located, so he

Above: Sean Graham Bookmakers of Dundalk, seen here in 1998 with Sean junior (left) and Brian Graham.

began by working alongside Peter Fitzsimons and through him he got to learn the ins and outs of the racecourse betting business. Meanwhile, he also operated at Belfast's greyhound track and built up a Starting Price business in a shop. He steadily built up the number of betting shops, mostly in the North, to a peak of fifty.

At last, in the early 1970s, he was able to acquire a Dublin address, and with it a bookmaker's licence. He became a generous race sponsor, both in the north and south of Ireland and in the UK, at top places like Leopardstown, the Curragh, Punchestown and Cheltenham, as well as all the smaller Irish tracks.

Brian has been 'making a book' since he was eighteen, when his father died aged only forty-six; it was a case of going into the family business or losing it. Brian had grown up embroiled in the bookmaking life and the rest he picked up as he went along.

'I wasn't really qualified for anything else,' he says. 'Ninety per cent of me has no regrets and perhaps ten per cent I wish I could have gone to college with my mates, I saw them enjoying university life for four years, having a good time. But then, I love what I do.'

It was a big learning curve at first and he remembers only too well one of his first 'huge mistakes'.

It was at Punchestown, and one particular punter had backed five losers.

'He was chasing his own money, and I laid £40,000 at 6-4, and I sat tight instead of laying it off, unfortunately.'

'Laying off' the money means 'divvying' the bet out with other bookmakers to ease the loss if the horse wins (because it is now spread between several individuals instead of one); of course, if it loses, then, by having 'laid off' much of the bet, the individual bookie has not gained as much as if he'd held on to the full wager.

The horse won, by a distance. And his name? *Carvill's Hill*, who was one of the top steeplechasers of his generation; he won eleven of his seventeen chases including a Welsh National, was second twice, unplaced once and fell three times, mostly for Jim Dreaper and latterly for Martin Pipe; he was injury-plagued and unlucky not to win a Cheltenham Gold Cup.

'The bookies' bad days stick in their minds more than the good,' Brian says, 'we see the racing from a different angle to the punters.'

Punchestown 2009 Festival, for example, saw the bookies' satchels being emptied as more and more people backed any horse ridden by Ruby Walsh – ten of them won!

Interviewed on television, Brian said, 'Nearly all the fancied horses are winning and the punters are winning, we are down. We had one punter place €6,000 cash on *Hurricane Fly* and then he put the winnings on *Master Minded* [who only won by a head]. The punters are latching on to Ruby, he usually hugs the rails.'

The recession was affecting the amount placed. 'What used to be €100 bets are now €20; a thousand has become five or six hundred.'

With Brian in the business are his sister, Claire, and his younger brothers, Gareth, Simon, Carl and Ronan. Only his twin, Sean, who started out in the family business, chose a different profession in the internet world.

Brian and his wife Zita have four children, three boys and a girl, ranging in age from six down to a few months old.

What Brian loves most about his job is the variety.

'There are never two days the same; I can be at Naas on Wednesday, Gowran on Thursday and then Friday I'll be working in the shop in Belfast.

'I'm meeting different people every day of the week, it keeps me on my toes.'

He loves being out in the fresh air at the race-meetings 'even when the weather is bad,' and he enjoys the 50,000 miles or so a year that he drives.

There is only one track in the whole of Ireland where he does not have a pitch (apart from Laytown's annual beach meeting).

'We don't go to Cork really because nine times out of ten it clashes with another meeting, and it is usually a one-day fixture – and our drive just to get there would be six hours.

'It is different at the Kerry tracks because they are usually at least three-day meetings so we stay down.'

Horseracing, as for so many others involved in it, is his hobby as well as his career.

'For instance, if it's my turn to give the baby his bottle in the middle of the night I turn on the racing channel on TV; I like all aspects of it.'

He considers *El Gran Senor* the best horse he has ever seen on the Flat for his scintillating win in the 1984 Irish Derby.

'I have never seen an easier winner in my life.'

For jumping, his choice is *Dawn Run*. 'When you're young you expect to see another one within five years, but it just doesn't happen.'

He adds, 'But what I love best is any runner of my mother's. She usually has one or two and breeds a few, it keeps her interested.'

The horse that has probably given the family most enjoyment of all is *Southern Vic*, owned by Mrs Graham, who ran in the 2009 Aintree Grand National.

Southern Vic, trained by Ted Walsh, finished best of the eleven-strong Irish contingent in

Below: Brenda Graham, widow of the founder of the bookmaking firm Sean Graham (here with jockey Ruby Walsh), loves having a runner, and has the consistent Southern Vic *in training with Ted Walsh.*

eighth place. He has been a model of reliability in his career, winning his second point-to-point by a distance, a maiden hurdle at the Leopardstown Christmas meeting and quickly followed that up with another hurdle win on the same course.

Already consistent, it was when he went chasing that he came into his own, very often with Ruby Walsh in the saddle. He has won five in all and placed in three; his first chase win was at the Galway October meeting where he beat *Slim Pickings* and went up a class when winning the Grade 1 novice chase at Leopardstown at Christmas. Victories followed at Naas twice and Navan.

Having a runner in the Grand National was an unforgettable experience.

'I loved the whole atmosphere, the feeling a part of it,' says Brian, who was off duty that day. 'The horse has taken us where we would not otherwise have been and Aintree was special, the whole thing.

'It was definitely a case of taking part rather than winning. After all, there will be thirty-nine losers but I'd say 90 per cent of those would have enjoyed the experience and been excited.'

Of his children, Michael, Thomas, Norah and Conor, he says, 'I wouldn't put them off coming into the business – but nor would I drag them in, it's for them to choose.'

Odds-on, I'd say. After all, it's in the blood.

INDEX